Christmas in Washington, D.C.

Christmas in Washington, D.C.

Christmas Around the World
From World Book

World Book, Inc.
a Scott Fetzer Company
Chicago

Christmas in Washington, D.C. was prepared by the Editorial and Art Departments of World Book, Inc.

Copyright © 1988 by World Book, Inc.
Merchandise Mart Plaza, Chicago, Illinois 60654

Printed in the United States of America.
ISBN 0-7166-0888-X
Library of Congress Catalog Card No. 88-50693
a/hh

Contents

A Capital Christmas

The ancient Romans had a minor god of gates and doors named Janus. His head featured two faces. One looked backward, and one looked forward. Washington is a Janus-faced kind of place. As the capital of the nation, it is immersed in history and tradition. And as the capital of the nation, it seethes with politics and the brokering of power. Tradition resists change; power thrives on it—one city, two faces. One looks

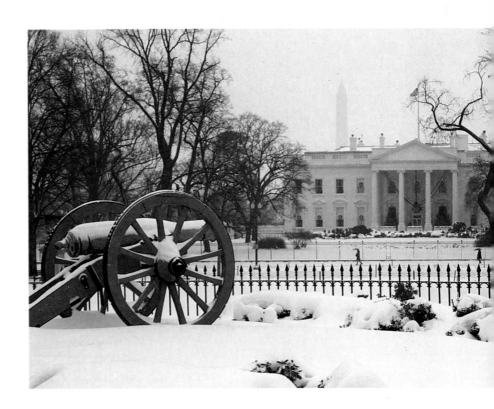

The Capitol tree (left) is seen against the Capitol's cast iron dome, completed in 1863. The White House, decorated for Christmas (right), is seen from Lafayette Square. The cannon was captured by Andrew Jackson in the War of 1812.

backward, and one looks forward. But, if it is
true that one needs to know the past to
understand the future, then a nation's capital
should have two faces.

In the United States, Christmas also has more
than one face. It is, first of all, a sacred
celebration of the birth of the Christ. It is also a
family celebration, an affirmation of kinship and
home. And in the United States, Christmas is
also something of a national holiday, complete
with an economy and economic indicators. The
varied faces of Christmas in America resist and
embrace change. They must. While the essential
nature and message of the Nativity of Jesus
remains constant, the other celebrations change,
exactly as the family and the nation change.

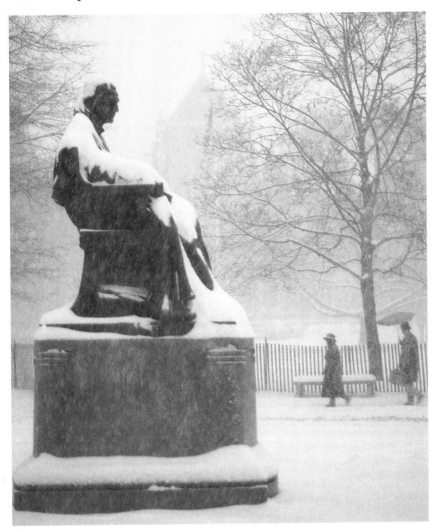

Christmas in Washington is a sacred celebration of the birth of Jesus; it is an affirmation of the family and home; but, above all, it is the story of a national celebration. A Christmas in Chicago is not very different from a Christmas in Atlanta or Boston or Sacramento. Christmas in Washington, however, is unique.

Officially, the government of the United States does not celebrate religious holidays. Unofficially, of course, it does. There is a national *Christmas* tree; there is a capitol *Christmas tree; there is a White House decked out for the holidays; there is Christmas on the National Mall, a holiday celebration not quite like any other in the world.*

Officially, the churches of Washington are exactly like churches in Chicago or Atlanta or Sacramento. Unofficially, certain churches in Washington are viewed as national institutions. And the celebration of the anniversary of the birth of Jesus in such a church is not quite like a Christmas service anywhere else.

College students, home for the holidays (below), stroll across the West Capitol Grounds. Narrow Georgetown streets become snowbound after a holiday storm (right). One of the oldest communities in North America, Georgetown was a thriving tobacco trading port before becoming part of the District of Columbia. The west front of the Capitol as seen from a detail of the Grant Memorial (far right). The Memorial, which stretches for 252 feet along the foot of Capitol Hill, was dedicated in 1922.

Washingtonians would agree that they share their city with the nation and the rest of the world. Thus, Christmas in their city is shared with the nation and the world. The National Christmas Tree is the nation's tree. Christmas at the White House is a symbol of Christmas at every American house. As we shall see, the National Mall is the nation's Main Street. And the Washington, or National, Cathedral, while an Episcopal church, is indeed a "house of prayer for all people."

At one o'clock on the afternoon of December 7, 1941,

Eleanor Roosevelt received luncheon guests at the White House. She announced that "the president would be unable to come down to luncheon." One of the guests, H.P. Hamlin, remembered that a flustered Mrs. Roosevelt had confided that "the news from Japan was very bad." At 9:30 the night before, the president had been called away from dinner to read intercepted telegrams that outlined Japan's formula for a "diplomatic Pacific settlement."

Franklin Delano Roosevelt addresses the nation, via radio, on Christmas Eve, 1941. To his right is British Prime Minister Winston Churchill. The first National Christmas Tree had just been lighted.

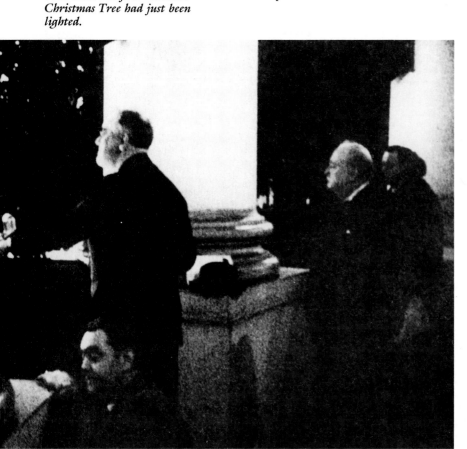

Directly above the Blue Room, where Mrs. Roosevelt was receiving, Franklin Roosevelt was eating lunch from a desktop tray in his study. At approximately 1:40 the telephone rang. Frank Knox, the secretary of the navy, had just received a radio message from Honolulu: "AIR RAID ON PEARL HARBOR THIS IS NOT A DRILL."

On Monday, December 8, Congress declared war on Japan. On December 11, Germany and Italy declared war on the United States. World War II had escalated to global proportions.

In those final days of 1941, tension filled the streets and offices of official Washington. Many believed the city would be bombed. A blackout was ordered. At the White House, a special detachment of military police was put on 24-hour duty. The military and the Secret Service demanded that additional measures be taken to protect the chief executive: machine guns on the White House roofs; bulletproof window glass; a sandbag barricade 15 feet high around the Executive Mansion and offices; a bomb shelter; and a White House repainted in standard Army Air Corps camouflage. Roosevelt balked at their demands. They also ordered that the Washington Community Christmas Tree, tra-

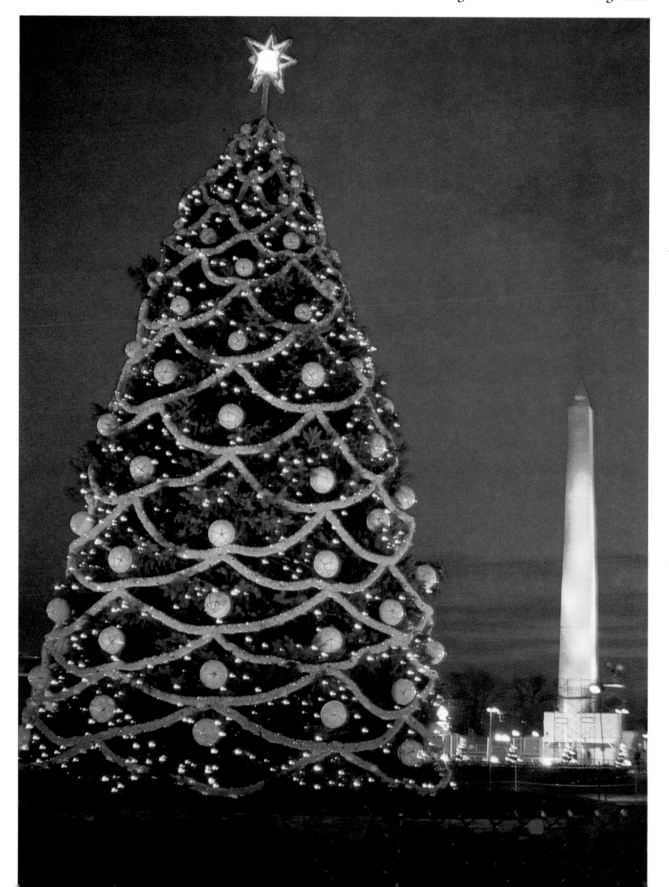

ditionally located near the White House and lighted by the president, be suspended for the duration. If Roosevelt balked at the serious measures, he bristled over the Christmas tree ban.

As a master politician, Franklin Roosevelt well understood the value of symbols. We were fighting a war to preserve our heritage; Christmas was part of that heritage. Besides, the president loved Christmas and Christmas trees. He would have the tree. The Secret Service refused. Roosevelt retorted that their attitude smacked of cowardice. The tree, they argued, would interfere with the civil defense of the city. Roosevelt was adamant. The Secret Service offered a compromise; there could be a tree, but no lights.

In the end, there was a tree. There were lights. And President Roosevelt participated in the lighting ceremony. He even renamed the tree. The Washington Community Christmas Tree became the National Christmas Tree. He did compromise to the extent that the tree was moved from Lafayette Park, which was public, to the south lawn of the White House, which was private although highly visible.

On December 24, 1941, President and Mrs. Roosevelt stood under the great, curving south portico of the White House. Next to the president stood British Prime Minister Winston Churchill, who had arrived that morning amid great secrecy. Because of the blackout, they could not see the 15,000 people standing outside the iron fence sur-

rounding the south lawn. The president pushed a button, which triggered a signal in a hole dug under the tree. Inside, an electrician threw a switch. And, suddenly, the tree was ablaze with thousands of lights. A kaleidoscope of color reflected across the facade of the old house and across the faces of the people. Spontaneously, they began to sing. Across the nation that Christmas Eve, millions of people listening over their radios heard Roosevelt and Churchill join in the caroling. Later, Churchill expressed to all Americans his comfort at sharing Christmas joys with them. But it was thoughts of children that inspired his message to Americans in 1941.

> . . . Let the children have their night of laughter . . . Let us grown-ups share . . . in their unstinted pleasures before we turn again to the stern tasks and the formidable years that lie before us, resolved that by our sacrifice and daring these same children shall not be robbed of their inheritance or denied their right to live in a free and decent world.

And so in the first fearful weeks of World War II, the National Christmas tree came to be. The idea, however, was conceived in 1923 by Frederick Feiker of the Society of Electrical Development, an organization promoting the use of electricity. Feiker convinced President Coolidge to participate in a tree-lighting ceremony. A large tree from Coolidge's native Vermont was erected on the Ellipse, a circular park that connects the White House to the Mall. Coolidge turned on the lights but, true to form, refused to speak.

The event was nearly canceled after a single year. In 1924, Coolidge protested the cutting of trees for Christmas. To save the Community Tree, Feiker arranged for a living tree to be planted on Sherman Square, east of the White House. Coolidge again participated in the lighting. This tree, however, did not live through the winter.

In Washington, politics permeates everything, including Christmas trees. While Feiker's Community Tree did become a tradition, it remained something of an orphan. It was, over the years, moved from the Ellipse, to Sherman Square, to Lafayette Park (north of the White House), to the south lawn, and back to the Ellipse. This shifting may have been due to politics—to pressures brought to bear on the president by conservation-minded citizens. When the nation was in a "conservation mood," a live tree was planted. The trouble with a permanent living tree was that it always died. This may have been bad luck or a matter of benign neglect. Washington, designed by Pierre L'Enfant in the late 18th century, is a city of formal squares and circles. A single, large evergreen does not well fit the character of L'Enfant's perfect little parks that circle the White House. Planting a tree to satisfy conservationists was easy enough; keeping it alive, however, was probably not much of a priority. When the next tree was planted,

it was probably moved to a new spot in the hope that, if it did survive, it might look a little less out of place during the 51 weeks that it was not decorated for Christmas.

By 1941, when Roosevelt rechristened the tree, the idea of a living tree was given up. In times of war, conservation becomes a moot point. And certainly no one wanted a fir tree growing in the center of the south lawn.

In 1954, the National Christmas Tree was moved permanently

The Capitol Christmas Tree, supplied to Congress by the U.S. Forest Service, is erected on the Capitol's west front terraces and is visible the full length of the Mall. (The west facade of the Capitol is currently undergoing restoration.)

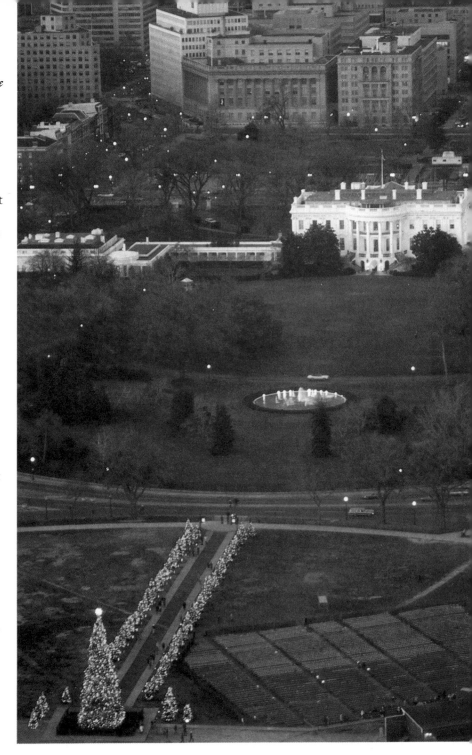

to the Ellipse. That year community leaders organized the Pageant of Peace, which was intended to serve as a symbol of the country's goal for international peace. The pageant was scheduled to begin with the tree lighting ceremony, which was moved forward by about a week at the request of President Eisenhower, who preferred to be home in Gettysburg before Christmas Eve. The Pageant of Peace, which continues today, includes nightly choral programs; an ever-burning Yule log; a life-sized Nativity scene; a herd of reindeer from the zoo; and 57 5-foot trees that represent the states, the District of Columbia, and the U.S. territories.

The Pageant of Peace inaugurated the era of really big National Christmas trees, which were annually donated by the different states. Each state, of course, vied to send a bigger and better tree. The record is held by South Dakota, which, in 1971, sent a 78-foot white spruce. Unfortunately, this tree was plagued by trouble. The train carrying it to Washington was derailed twice. During the decorating, high winds blew the tree down. Finally, during the ceremony, a driving rain drove the audience home. Understandably, trees as large as this were difficult to transport and prepare. This fact coupled with renewed pressure from conservationists ended the era of the "great" trees. The last was seen in 1972, which was about the time that "conservation" became known as "ecology." With the nation again interested in conservation, the

National Tree was again a living tree. And, again, the living tree died. Finally, the National Park Service attacked the Christmas tree "problem." In 1978, after a determined search, a park ranger found the perfect tree—a 30-foot blue spruce growing in the yard of the Myers family of York, Pennsylvania. It had been Mrs. Myers' Mother's Day gift 15 years earlier. A price of $1,500 was negotiated.

The tree was carefully uprooted, transported, and replanted on the Ellipse. It continues to thrive today. The permanent National Tree grows just east of the north entrance to the Ellipse and is part of a border of elms that frames this large, oval parade ground. Thus, the tree does not intrude upon the symmetry of L'Enfant's President's Park. One of the most carefully tended trees in the world, the National Christmas Tree should survive for generations and reach a height equal to those giant trees of the 50's and 60's.

Although the Park Service cares for the tree, it is decorated by General Electric Company engineers, who design the decorations beginning in early fall. Each year a new theme and new colors are chosen. Everything must be ready by the last Thursday that is at least one week before Christmas—the official day of the lighting ceremony. Meanwhile, the Park Service erects a stage for the ceremony and the nightly choral programs. Since 1981, President Reagan, heeding Secret Service advice, has lit the tree and delivered his Christmas message via video hookup from inside the White House. Nevertheless, throngs of tourists and Washingtonians gather on the Ellipse for the opening of the Pageant of Peace. The musical programs are also well attended through New Year's Eve.

Not all Washingtonians, however, are thrilled with the decorations of the National Tree or with the hoopla that surrounds it. A staff writer for The Washington Post described it as "somehow dull. It lacks vitality. It looks like something a major corporation would design." He suggested that Washingtonians switch their loyalty to the Capitol Christmas Tree. This tree, which is erected on the west lawn of the Capitol, is what the National Tree used to be—an immense, cut tree, randomly decorated with thousands of lights and ornaments that are reused year after year. The tree,

which is usually about 60 feet tall, is supplied by the U.S. Forest Service. It is decorated by the staff of the architect of the Capitol with 5,000 lights and innumerable, homemade bells, stars, and angels. There is no great pomp surrounding the Capitol Tree, but the people come to watch the glitter of its lights and listen to it "sing," that is, listen to the bulbs and ornaments rattle and jingle in the raw wind that blows around Capitol Hill on blustery, December nights.

North of the National Christmas Tree stands the White House.

Completed in 1800, it is the oldest public building in Washington. The only president who did not live in the house was George Washington, who personally approved architect James Hoban's plans. From mid-December through the new year, the White House is lavishly decorated for Christmas and is visited by nearly 100,000 tourists and guests. The view of the White House from the Ellipse includes all of the south lawn, nearly 18 acres, and the south facade, graced by a col-

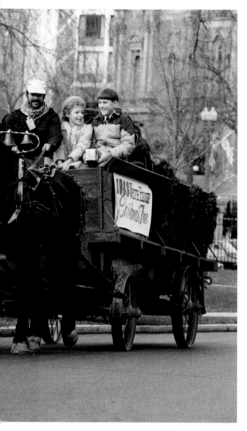

The President's Christmas tree (insert), which is donated by the National Christmas Tree Association, is transported to the White House in a horse-drawn wagon. The East Room of the White House (left) is lavishly decorated for Christmas. Through the years this room, perhaps the most historic in the nation, has been the scene of every kind of event: weddings, funerals, state dinners for visiting royalty, the presentation of Indian chiefs in full regalia, and even sumo wrestling matches.

umned, three-story portico. Under the carriage lights on either side of the portico entrance stand two lighted, conical evergreens, seven feet in height. Evergreen roping drapes the porch railing and the Truman Balcony, as well as down the two, curving staircases, which connect the first floor with the south lawn. A wreath hangs at each of the three levels of the south portico. Through the curved panes of glass in the center window one can see the White House Christmas tree, which stands in the center of the Blue Room.

Public tours of the White House are conducted on Tuesdays through Saturdays, from 10 A.M. until noon. However, during the Christmas season the residence is also open to the public at night. These "candlelight" tours were begun by Pat Nixon. Popular with both tourists and Washingtonians, the candlelight tours have become a traditional part of the Washington Christmas season.

If one were to take a candlelight tour, one would begin at the visitor's entrance of the East Wing, which was constructed in 1902 and enlarged in 1942. As each visitor enters, he or she receives a small booklet containing a message from the first lady and a description of White House Christmas decorations. Inside the East Wing Garden Room is a large cone-shaped tree made from pink and white poinsettias. Along the colonnade, built on the foundations of a similar structure designed by Thomas Jefferson, evergreen wreaths hang in the windows. Potted white poinsettia

plants line this corridor. The way is lighted by white candles, which stand on teakwood candlesticks made by resident craftspeople. Also along the way is a display of 34 official White House Christmas cards; the first was sent by President and Mrs. Eisenhower in 1953.

At the end of the colonnade, one finds oneself in the ground floor corridor. Before 1902, this area contained kitchens, pantries, and the furnace and coal rooms. Overhead is a vaulted ceiling constructed of stone, which originally supported the house above.

During the War of 1812, the British burned the White House. To save time and money during the reconstruction, the interior was rebuilt with wooden supports. (The original construction, supervised by George Washington, was all masonry and much superior.) Over the next 120 years, water pipes, gas lines, furnace flues, and electrical wiring were cut through timbers. In 1902, the house's principal staircase was removed to enlarge the State Dining Room. In the process, load-bearing walls were removed; the weight of the unsupported load was then simply shifted to existing timbers. On top of this, in 1927, a third floor, partially constructed of concrete, was added.

By 1948, the White House was in danger of collapsing. In August of that year, a leg of Margaret Truman's piano crashed through the second floor, causing the ceiling below to fall. Between 1948 and 1952, the entire inner structure of the house was removed and rebuilt in steel and concrete.

The White House crèche, or Nativity scene, is placed in a window alcove in the East Room. It is seen here from the Cross Hall, which is decorated with poinsettias and evergreen wreaths and festoons. The balcony on the left is a landing of the Grand Staircase, which is used by the president and first lady on state occasions.

Subbasements were dug, and a considerable number of service rooms were added.

Truman insisted that as much of the old as possible be saved. Along the ground floor corridor are a number of rooms paneled in pine, which was salvaged from the timbers that once supported the old house. The walls of this hallway are hung with portraits of first ladies, which during an evening tour, are lighted by candles.

A broad flight of stairs leads from the ground floor corridor to the first, or state, floor. At the top of the stairs, one turns to the right and enters the East Room, the largest and most formal of the state rooms. It appears almost empty, the far corners lost in shadows. Under the three great chandeliers, which were installed in 1902, six 21-foot and two 12-foot blue spruce trees are arranged along the walls. They are decorated with tiny, white lights, silver snowflakes, simulated snow, icicles, and tinsel. Garlands of mixed greenery are suspended by red ribbons around the gilded mirrors, which reflect and end-

lessly multiply the images of lighted candles set in candelabra, which rest on the four fireplace mantels. In the center of the long east wall a crèche is set in a gold-draped doorway. The crèche, or Nativity scene, has been displayed every Christmas since 1967, when it was donated to the White House by Mrs. Charles W. Englehard, Jr. The 47 figures, made of carved wood and terra cotta, were crafted in Naples, Italy, in the 18th century. The figures, which range in height from 12 to 18 inches, depict the Holy Family, the three kings, their attendants, shepherds, angels, cherubs, and animals associated with the Nativity story. (The White House crèche is pictured on the 1988 Christmas Around the World Advent calendar.)

The East Room, designed by Hoban as the "public audience room," has been the scene of an extraordinary variety of events: Abigail Adams hung her wash here because she thought it indelicate to expose the presidential linen to public scrutiny; Thomas Jefferson and Meriwether Lewis planned the exploration of the West in the room; Union troops were billeted here during the Civil War; Teddy Roosevelt's boys roller-skated across the parquet floor; their father staged sumo wrestling matches on it; daughters of Presidents U.S. Grant, Theodore Roosevelt, Woodrow Wilson, and Lyndon Johnson were married in the East Room; and seven presidents, including Abraham Lincoln, Franklin Delano Roosevelt, and John Kennedy, laid in state here. It is, perhaps, the most historic room in America.

From the East Room, the tour moves west into the Green Room, a formal parlor decorated in the Sheraton style of 1800-1810. The room is lighted by candles set on various side tables and on the white marble mantel, which was purchased by President Monroe in 1817. Opposite the fireplace is an arrangement of two armchairs, a settee, and a drop-leaf table, all by the American cabinetmaker Duncan Phyfe. On

President and Mrs. Reagan (above) *decorate their Christmas tree in the second floor center hall, which is part of the private quarters of the White House. Members of the White House staff* (right) *decorate the North Entrance for Christmas. The year was 1938; the low ramp leading to the door accommodated President Roosevelt's wheelchair.*

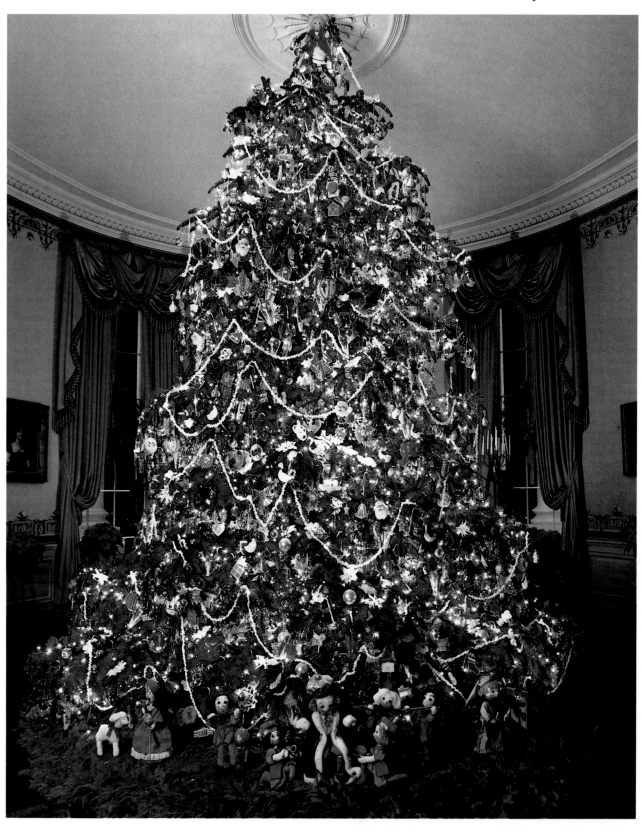

the table are two lighted candles set in silver sticks that were used in this room by Dolley Madison. Between the candles is a silver-plated coffee urn that was owned by John Adams, who considered it one of his "most prized possessions."

The Green Room is decorated for Christmas with greenery, holly, and white tulips arranged in bowls from the White House china collection. Double-faced wreaths hang from red bows and streamers in the deep window reveals. The walls of the room are hung with green, watered silk, first used in 1962 by Jacqueline Kennedy. (For an illustration of the Green Room, see the White House article in *The World Book Encyclopedia.*)

Thomas Jefferson used the Green Room for dining. In the spirit of democracy, he insisted upon a round table so there would be no head, and he banished all servants during meals. Food and service dishes were placed in warming cabinets from which the president and his guests took turns serving. The resulting privacy and informality promoted frank and lively conversation, which Jefferson, who understood the isolation of the presidency, appreciated.

Beyond the Green Room is the Blue Room, which is "elliptical" or oval in shape. Presidents have traditionally used the room to receive guests. During the Christmas season, the crystal chandelier is removed to make way for the White House Christmas tree, which usually stands 17 to 18 feet high.

The White House State Dining Room is decorated for Christmas with evergreen roping and poinsettias. The Healy portrait of Lincoln hangs above a mantel embellished with buffalo heads. Installed during the Theodore Roosevelt Administration, the mantel was lost during the Truman renovation, but reproduced at President Kennedy's suggestion.

The tree is decorated with thousands of tiny, white lights and a variety of ornaments, which change from year to year. During the Reagan administration, White House trees have been highly traditional. One year the tree was trimmed with babies-breath, dusty miller, and other dried wild flowers, along with 150 angels made from pine cones, nuts, and dried thistles. Another year Mrs. Reagan chose a Mother Goose theme; the tree was decorated with miniature geese,

A Civil War-era political cartoon shows President Lincoln offering Christmas dinner to reluctant guests. The empty chairs represent the Confederate states that have left the Union.

gold-foil snowflakes, and wooden cookies. Another tree, hung with Victorian dolls in period costumes, had a turn-of-the-century flavor; the dolls were designed and dressed by the White House flower shop staff. More recently, the tree was laden with miniature musical instruments, musical notes, and rolled sheet music tied with ribbons. Nancy Reagan has personally decorated White House trees with the help of residents of Second Genesis, a drug rehabilitation center.

Each year the White House tree is donated to the president by the National Christmas Tree Association's champion grower. It is ceremoniously transported to the White House on a horse-drawn wagon.

The Blue Room is decorated in the Empire style popular when the house was rebuilt after the fire of 1814. At that time, President Monroe ordered new furnishings for the Executive Mansion. Included in this purchase were 38 pieces of gilded furniture, made by Bellangé of Paris. This suite remained in the Blue Room until 1860 when President Buchanan's niece, Harriet Lane, sold it at auction. In 1902, Charles McKim, architect for the Roosevelt restoration, reproduced the Bellangé suit from photographs and a painting. In 1962, an original Bellangé chair was found and acquired by the White House. Since then a sofa and six more chairs have been returned to the house. Today, the Blue Room is furnished with a combination of the originals and the 1902 reproductions. Traditionally, a round table has been placed in the center of the room. Used as protection, the president stood to one side of the table to avoid being crushed during large, public receptions. Until 1930, presidents received and shook hands with literally thousands of people on New Year's Day.

The next room on the candlelight tour is the Red Room, a formal parlor of the American Empire period (1810-1830). The walls are hung with red satin twill, trimmed at the cornice with a red and gold border. The furniture is American Empire upholstered in red and gold damask. (For an illustration of the Red Room, see the White House article in *The World Book Encyclopedia.*)

For Christmas, the Red Room is decorated with arrangements of evergreen, holly, and white narcissus and amaryllis arranged in gilded, silver bowls from the Biddle vermeil collection, which was donated to the White House in 1956. Evergreen wreaths hang from red bows in the windows.

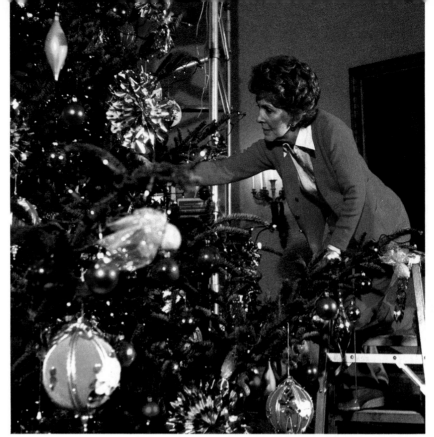

Mrs. Reagan has personally decorated the White House Christmas tree with the aid of residents of Second Genesis, a drug rehabilitation center.

The Red Room was used by Dolley Madison for her popular Wednesday evening receptions. A painting of her hangs in the room. Abraham and Mary Lincoln also frequently used the Red Room for informal entertaining. A contemporary noted that it was furnished and decorated with pieces "very ancient, being bought or presented during Monroe's and Madison's Administrations." The fireplace mantel, upon which candles burn, is one of those "very ancient" pieces.

The Red Room opens directly into the State Dining Room, which is spectacularly decorated for Christmas. The table is laid with gold candelabra, burning red candles, and the Monroe plateau, a mirrored, gilt centerpiece, which is one of the most treasured pieces in the house. Purchased by Monroe, the plateau has been in continuous use since 1817. (For a complete illustration of the State Dining Room, see the White House article in *The World Book Encyclopedia.*) Also on the table are boxwood topiary, trimmed with twisted red cord and gold bead strings. On one of the console tables is a gingerbread house, 3 feet high and weighing 45 pounds. The house was made by Hans Raffert, an assistant executive chef, who has baked one each year since 1969. The gingerbread house is decorated with traditional German cookies, candy canes, hard candies, royal icing, gingerbread dough, and sugary fallen snow. Hansel and Gretel, a witch, and a snowman, all made of marzipan, stand in the house's snow-filled yard. (The gingerbread house is pictured on page 64 of *Christmas in Washington, D.C.*)

Above the dining room fireplace, the frame of Healy's portrait of Lincoln is draped with an immense garland trimmed with long, red ribbons. The mantel, embellished with buffalo heads, is a reproduction of one installed by Theodore Roosevelt in 1902. During the Truman renovation, the original was removed and lost. In 1962, President Kennedy suggested that a copy of the buffalo mantel be reinstalled. Carved into the mantel is an inscription written by John Adams on his second night in the Executive Mansion: "I Pray Heaven to Bestow the Best of Blessings on THIS HOUSE and on All that shall hereafter Inhabit it. May none but Honest and Wise Men ever rule under this Roof."

From the State Dining Room the tour moves onto the Cross Hall. In the two niches are trees decorated with gold balls and snowflakes, gold-wrapped walnuts, papier-mâché angels, and white candles. Suspended with red ribbon above two pier tables are large evergreen wreaths trimmed with pine cones and red berries.

The Cross Hall is separated from the Entrance Hall by a colonnade of paired marble columns. Beyond it, garlands trimmed with red ribbons are hung over the pier mirrors that reflect the grand staircase on the other side of the hall. One leaves through the north door, which opens under the north portico. The exterior door is flanked by 16-foot, lighted fir trees. The lantern hanging from the ceiling of the portico and its five supporting chains are wrapped with evergreen roping.

It is a short walk down the curving driveway. Overhead, the branches of bare elms rustle in a slight breeze. At the gates on Pennsylvania Avenue, one turns for a final look. In each of the sixteen windows, eight on either side of the portico, hangs a wreath lighted by a single candle.

The White House is a unique place, neither private house nor public office. Throughout its 188-year history, it has continually changed, reflecting the changing character of the nation. Between 1800 and 1860, when the nation was primarily agrarian, the White House was something of a grand country house. Christmas celebrations in the Executive Mansion have also reflected the changing times and the people who lived through those times.

The first presidents were either Virginians or New Englanders. Most Virginians, due to their English and Anglican heritage, celebrated Christmas with feasting and revelry characteristic of old, feudal traditions. We know that one Christmas at Mount Vernon was celebrated with dancing, games, and a great feast that included five kinds of meat—beef, turkey, veal, duck, and ham; vegetables and several kinds of fruits and nuts—oranges, apples, almonds, figs, and raisins; and such desserts as sweet potato pudding and plum pudding, served with jellies; the meal was washed down with wines and whiskey punches. It's likely that the young men, probably after sampling the punches, continued to celebrate by stepping outside to shoot off their muskets. That, too, was a traditional part of the day.

President Grant receives King Kalakaua of the Hawaiian Islands at a Christmas reception. The drawing accurately depicts the East Room as remodeled by President and Mrs. Grant in what has since been described as "steamboat gothic."

The first inhabitants of the President's House were not, however, the Washingtons, but the Adamses, New Englanders of Puritan stock. The Puritans, a sect that grew out of the English Reformation, viewed Christmas with some suspicion. To them, holiday feasting and merrymaking seemed inappropriate, if not downright pagan. In certain New England colonies, Christmas was even banned by law. Christmas for the Adamses was likely more staid and reserved than a Christmas celebrated by the Virginian presidents.

The first Christmas celebration in the White House was a party held, in 1800, for the Adamses' granddaughter, 4-year-old Susanna. The Adamses had only moved in a month before. The rooms, largely unfinished, were cold, damp, and drafty. The only source of warmth was the fireplaces, which were numerous but incapable of warming the immense, high-ceilinged rooms. Mrs. Adams burned 20 cords of wood in each fireplace in an attempt to dry out the drafty house before that Christmas. Still, most guests, who were unable to conceal their discomfort, left early. (The Adamses were also considered somewhat chilly hosts.) While the children did not seem to mind the cold, the party was not altogether a success. Susanna bit the nose from a playmate's new wax doll after the envious playmate had smashed her new doll dishes. The president had to mediate a peace.

Thomas Jefferson also loved having his six grandchildren at the White House. One Christmas he held a party for them and 100 friends. A widower, Jefferson asked Dolley Madison to act as hostess. Unlike Abigail Adams, Mrs. Madison loved to entertain. There is no record that guests left early. Before it was over, Jefferson put his pet bird through its repertoire of tricks and played the violin while the children danced.

Mrs. Madison, as first lady, also hosted the first truly grand Christmas party at the White House. One of the guests was writer Washington Irving, who later noted that Dolley wore a bright purple dress, pearls, many bracelets, and the feathered turban that was her trademark. The State Dining Room was lighted by over 100 candles, and there was a waiter, probably a rented slave, for each guest. After dinner, the indomitable Mrs. Madison managed to charm her guests, many of whom were political enemies, into playing games, singing, and dancing.

Through the center window is the White House Christmas tree. Directly above is the oval room where Franklin Pierce probably placed the White House's first tree.

A late 1880's engraving shows guests arriving for a Christmas reception. Carriages drove through the portico. The lamps on the columns and ornamental fence, installed in 1833, were removed during the 1902 renovation.

President Hoover lights the Washington Community Christmas Tree in 1931. Mrs. Hoover and the President's grandchildren stand to his right.

the room and struck its target, it broke open, showering snow and candy kisses over little heads.

One Christmas morning, President Jackson woke to find a filled stocking hanging from the fireplace mantel. "Old Hickory" openly wept as he examined the contents, gifts and trinkets left by his adopted family. Jackson had been an orphan. As a child, he had never received a gift, nor even known that such a day as Christmas existed. Each Christmas, Jackson carried gifts and treats to orphanages in and around Washington. He stated that it was important "to begin our holiday by remembering the little ones who have no mothers or fathers to brighten life for them."

The first Christmas tree in the White House was decorated by Franklin Pierce in 1853. Pierce may have been trying to cheer his wife Jane, who became a recluse after the death of her only child. The boy died when the train carrying the president-elect and his family to Washington derailed. In 1853 the Christmas tree was a novelty in this country. The custom was brought to America by German immigrants, perhaps as early as the 18th century; it did not gain wide acceptance, however, until Godey's Lady's Book, in 1850, published an engraving of Queen Victoria's tree at Buckingham Palace. The first White House tree was probably a small affair placed on a table in one of the second floor parlors.

It is not known if the Lincoln's had a Christmas tree in the White House. It is known, how-

President Andrew Jackson, also a widower, disliked being alone. Living with him were Jack and Emily Donelson, his beloved wife Rachel's niece and nephew, and their children. To entertain the children, Jackson invited 100 young Washingtonians for a Christmas "frolic in the East Room." After a supper, a great pyramid of decorated snowballs was dismantled from the center of the dining table and passed out to the children. Led by the president, the youngsters marched back into the East Room for a snowball fight. As each ball of starch-coated cotton sailed across ever, that on Christmas Day 1864, Tad Lincoln invited a gang of street urchins into the White House kitchen for dinner. When the appalled cook refused to feed them, Tad ran to his father. Although busy with guests, President Lincoln followed the boy downstairs to the kitchen and ordered the cook to serve the boys turkey dinners.

It was not unusual for Tad Lincoln to beg his father's intervention. (Everyone in the White House, except President and Mrs. Lincoln, thought Tad a spoiled brat.) During an earlier Christmas season, he interrupted a cabinet meeting when he discovered that a turkey, which he considered his pet, was going to be killed for the

president's Christmas dinner. Passionately insisting that "Jack" was a good turkey, Tad implored his father to pardon the bird. Lincoln, who could deny Tad nothing, relented, and "Jack" became a familiar sight parading around the south lawn.

The next recorded appearance of a White House Christmas tree was in 1889. President and Mrs. Harrison staged a tree-trimming party that included their children, grandchildren, and the White House staff, all of whom received gifts. The tree was placed in the second floor, oval library. In 1895, President Cleveland had his White House tree wired for electric lights, an operation performed by an electrician

that cost as much as a dollar a bulb. A tree in the White House became a tradition, that is, until Teddy Roosevelt became president.

Theodore Roosevelt, a staunch conservationist, decided that American forests were threatened by the cutting of trees for Christmas. To set an example, he forbade a tree in the White House. His sons, Archie and Quentin, however, smuggled one upstairs and hid it in their bedroom closet. On Christmas morning, the boys marched the family into their room, unveiled the tree, and offered everyone a gift. The president was not amused. After the holiday, the boys were sent to Gifford Pinchot, the country's foremost conservationist, to learn a lesson. The president's scheme backfired when Pinchot announced that the prudent cutting of smaller trees for Christmas could actually be helpful to the growth of forests. Pinchot and the National Forest Service also used the occasion to publicize the idea that growing Christmas trees might be a good way for farmers to utilize otherwise untillable land. But, Roosevelt, on principle, continued to ban White House Christmas trees, while ignoring his sons' "closet" trees.

President Coolidge, who began the tradition of lighting what became the National Christmas Tree, also initiated the singing of carols under the north portico of the White House. In 1923, the choir of the First Congregational Church was invited by Mrs. Coolidge, who loved music, to sing carols following the Christmas

Eve tree-lighting ceremony. The public was admitted to the north grounds and encouraged to sing along. Several days before the ceremony, the words to the carols had been printed in the newspaper with the suggestion that they be clipped and brought along with a flashlight. Separated from the tree-lighting ceremony, the carol sing-along has been practiced irregularly since the days of Coolidge. Lady Bird Johnson, in particular, encouraged it.

The most exciting Christmas Eve in White House history was probably December 24, 1929. During a party for the Hoover's grandchildren, it was discovered that the West Wing was on fire. All the men quietly excused themselves and rushed to the fire. Under the president's direction, papers, files, books, paintings, and even office furniture were saved from the flames that, eventually, gutted the office wing. No one was hurt, not even a puppy that was hidden in one of the offices. It was the president who remembered and ordered the rescue of the dog, which was a Christmas gift for an aid's son. Meanwhile, Mrs. Hoover kept the party going, calmly moving the children to the Christmas tree where she engaged them with stories.

As planned, the Hoovers hosted a dinner for 50 guests the following day. Each place at the table was set with either a bell or a brass candlestick. After dinner, President Hoover and his granddaughter led the guests on a march through the darkened parlors on the state floor. The men

The Harry Truman family celebrate Christmas in Blair House while the White House was being rebuilt. The Trumans moved into a White House in such bad shape that a leg of Margaret Truman's piano crashed through the floor.

carried the candles, the ladies rang the bells, and everyone sang carols.

Of all the first families that have lived in the White House, probably none have enjoyed Christmas more than the Franklin Roosevelts. Henrietta Nesbitt, the family's long-time cook and housekeeper, claimed that it was Eleanor Roosevelt's favorite time of the year, "when she seemed most happy." The first lady enjoyed shopping and searching for Christmas gifts throughout the year. She loved finding the perfect present for everyone, and she bought gifts for an extraordinary number of people—family, friends, her staff, the president's staff, the White House staff, even the house plumbers, electricians, and policemen. From year to year she kept running lists so that no gifts were repeated two years in a row. In October of each year, she took over a storage room on the third floor as her "toy room."

Here, she stockpiled and eventually wrapped all the gifts. On the Sunday nearest to Christmas, the President and Mrs. Roosevelt personally greeted staff members and their families and passed out gifts from under a huge tree set in the East Room.

The East Room tree, which was constantly pushed into or out of an alcove to accommodate Mrs. Roosevelt's various Christmas activities, was lighted with electric bulbs. But, the family tree, upstairs, was lighted with candles. Both the president and first lady claimed that Christmas was not Christmas without "the smell of hot evergreen." The fire marshall protested, but the president had his own way. Both Eleanor and Franklin insisted that Christmas in "this home away from home" must conform to Hyde Park traditions. Everything was done as it had always been done, and every year after Christmas Eve dinner, four generations

President and Mrs. Eisenhower (above) are surrounded by family and friends during Christmas dinner in the State Dining Room. Mamie Eisenhower so loved to decorate that she once put up 26 trees. A collection of White House Christmas cards (below) is displayed on the ground floor corridor during the holidays. Official White House Christmas cards were first mailed during the Eisenhower Administration.

of Roosevelts gathered around the fire in the president's oval study to listen to FDR read Dickens' *A Christmas Carol.* He knew most of it by heart and, over the years, worked up an "interpretation" that included a series of frightening ghosts.

Mamie Eisenhower staged some of the most spectacular Christmases that have ever taken place in the White House. As a cou-

ple, the Eisenhowers lived longer in the White House than in any other house; to Mamie Eisenhower, the White House was home. She also "simply loved to decorate." In 1959, she scattered 26 trees through the house, including one in the laundry. She had loudspeakers rigged up in the East Room, from which carols could be heard throughout the house. And she surrounded her-

Children's Christmas parties are a White House tradition that dates back to 1800, when John and Abigail Adams held a party for their granddaughter Susanna. Mrs. Reagan (left) hosts a party in the East Room for the children of diplomats. Mrs. Kennedy (insert) shows children the White House tree in the Blue Room. Mrs. Kennedy also gave White House Christmas parties for handicapped children.

self with friends and family, especially grandchildren, during the holidays. Like Mrs. Roosevelt, Mrs. Eisenhower's favorite time of the year was Christmas.

Aside from the family celebrations that take place during the Christmas holidays, there are many official gatherings and parties planned each year. One party, for the sons and daughters of diplomats, has been held for over 25 years. More than 350 children attend. The guests represent more than 75 countries, and many of the children come attired in native costumes. They are well entertained by cartoon characters, as well as by public personalities. Actress Helen Hayes has attended and performed *A Christmas Carol* for the children.

There is also a customary party for the children of White House staff members. First Lady Jacqueline Kennedy began the now annual Christmas party for disadvantaged children—following a tradition that dates back to Jackson and, of course, to little Tad Lincoln. In 1981, Nancy Reagan hosted yet another holiday party for children; this one for 178 hearing-impaired children.

Of course children are not the only guests at White House Christmas events. Mrs. Gerald Ford once commented that the holidays seemed to be a season of "continual parties." President and Mrs. Ford, who loved to dance, hosted "an honest-to-goodness ball" in the Blue Room.

Although the Jimmy Carter family always returned to Plains, Georgia, for Christmas, they made certain to wish their staff and members of Congress a joyous holiday season. In the weeks before Christmas, the Carters hosted as many as 15 parties, including a grand Christmas ball for the members of Congress and

President Johnson and Lady Bird Johnson entertain West German Chancellor Ludwig Erhard with Christmas carols on the South Portico—a White House tradition begun by Grace Coolidge.

34

their spouses—1,000 guests in all. It was fortunate that President Truman had the floors reinforced with steel and concrete.

When the White House was reopened after the 1948-1952 renovations, many people, including Eleanor Roosevelt, felt that the rich patina of age, of history, had been wiped away. It was all too clean, too perfect. President Truman, who took great pride in the house, was perhaps stung by their words. While retaining as much of the old as possible, he had rebuilt the house to last for centuries—time enough for the house to again acquire the patina of times past. The 100,000 people who visit the house during the Christmas season are each a witness and contributor to that richness of history.

In the days before World War II, Washington was thought by many to be a provincial kind of place,

During the holidays, the Kennedy Center for the Performing Arts is busy with Christmas activities and programs, including dancing in the Grand Foyer on New Year's Eve.

more a sleepy, southern town than a world capital. Temporary residents bemoaned the lack of culture, and embassy officials, especially Europeans, considered Washington a "hardship posting." These attitudes have, of course, changed. As the United States became a world power, its capital became the center of that power; a place that attracted, rather than repelled. And as the city became more important internationally, its cultural life blossomed. The Smithsonian grew until its combined facilities were internationally recognized as one of the world's finest museum complexes. In 1971, the John F. Kennedy Center for the Performing Arts opened its doors, at once making Washington an important center for theater, opera, film, and symphonic music.

At Christmastime, activity at the Kennedy Center is intense; programs are extraordinary in quality, variety, and number. Each year the National Symphony performs Handel's *Messiah*, and the Choral Arts Society of Washington performs seasonal music from a variety of periods. This concert concludes with the audience joining the chorus in the singing of familiar carols, all accompanied by the house's magnificent organ.

Another sing-along at the Kennedy Center joins an audience of 2,700 people, the Paul Hill Cho-

The Shiloh Choir entertains Washington office workers with holiday carols in the courtyard of the old Pension Building. From 1885 to 1926 payments to Civil War veterans went out from the offices along the galleries open to the courtyard. Today, the structure houses the National Building Museum and is open to the public.

rale, and the Holiday Festival Orchestra for a mass rendition of the *Messiah*. People queue up for the free "Sing-Along Messiah" tickets early in the morning, as all seats are generally taken within 90 minutes of the opening of the box office.

The Kennedy Center also offers holiday candlelight concerts, gospel concerts, and theater programs for children—a favorite is "Dick Whittington and His Cat." A Hanukkah concert is usually presented—often with the Shir Chadash Chorale performing an international repertoire of Jewish songs.

Another annual Center event is the singing Christmas tree. One hundred Greenville, South Carolina, high school students, robed in green and red, sing from a 24-foot, 7-level tree-shaped structure, around which more students perform country dances.

A most unusual event is the "Tuba Christmas." Because of the presence of the many U.S. service bands, Washington has the nation's highest concentration of tuba players. For over 20 years, they have gathered at Christmas-

time to delight listeners with holiday music in the low register. Any tuba player, amateur as well as professional, may participate.

From 10 A.M. to 3 P.M. on Christmas Eve, the Kennedy Center is the scene of another annual event: a live radio broadcast, hosted by a local station, that features a wide assortment of musical entertainment—from the Washington Mormon Choir to jazz guitarist Charlie Byrd. The program is free, and members of the audience are allowed to come and go at will.

While traveling troupes often perform Tchaikovsky's *The Nutcracker* at the Kennedy Center, Washington natives are partial to their own ballet company's production. Presented since 1961 at the Lisner Auditorium, *The Nutcracker* has become for many families a tradition that now spans three generations.

While the Kennedy Center offers the widest variety of holiday programs, Christmas events are presented all over the city—in churches, private homes, and even office buildings. At Constitution Hall, U.S. Army and

Navy bands offer special concerts. At the Capital Children's Museum, such puppet shows as "Babes in Toyland" delight young audiences. And at the National Theatre, a holiday tree lighting party, with music and dancing, is staged for the city's children.

Washington is a city where history and tradition are omnipresent. As a result, old buildings do not generally get torn down. They languish for a generation or two while committees debate their merit, both historic and artistic. A new generation then "discovers" and restores the old, utilizing their spaces in ways never dreamed of by the builders. Thus, the old Pension Building became the National Building Museum. Its immense atrium, which once housed files on Civil War veterans, now provides a kind of all-purpose space where, during the holidays, musical programs are presented for the enjoyment of office workers. The Old Post Office, a huge, Victorian pile on Pennsylvania Avenue that was, for three generations, considered an eyesore, has become a shopping mall, as well as home to some of the city's liveliest nightspots. Here, each Christmas season, musicians, jugglers, and singing toy soldiers entertain shoppers. Another "rehab," Georgetown's Old Stone House, built in 1765, is now the scene of annual Christmas chamber concerts.

One of the city's most beloved Christmas traditions is played out in what is, perhaps, the city's

Attending a performance of Tchaikovsky's **The Nutcracker,** *either at the Kennedy Center or at George Washington University's Lisner Auditorium, has become a traditional outing for many Washington families.*

Dickens' **A Christmas Carol** *is presented each December at Ford's Theatre, which was closed the night Lincoln was assassinated and was not reopened, as a theater, for 103 years.*

strangest and most tragic building. Dickens' classic *A Christmas Carol,* a story of bitterness, ghosts, and spiritual redemption, is presented annually at Ford's Theatre, a place of both bitterness and renewal.

Originally a Baptist church, the building was completed in 1839, four years before the publication of *A Christmas Carol.* In 1861, the church was remodeled into an opera house. It burned in 1862 and was, in 1863, rebuilt as a theater. On the night of April 14, 1865, John Wilkes Booth stole into the presidential box during a presentation of *Our American Cousin,* a play solely remembered for this one night's production. Using a derringer, Booth shot Abraham Lincoln and dramatically leaped onto the stage, breaking his leg in the process. In the wake of this tragedy, Ford's Theatre closed, seemingly forever.

During the 1870's, the building was converted into government offices. In June of 1893, the interior collapsed; 22 people were killed; 68 more were injured. Haunted by tragedy, the building was again closed. It sat empty for nearly another 40 years.

In 1932, Ford's Theatre reopened as a museum, housing the famous Oldroyd collection of Lincolniana. Among the relics were the flag and the spur that caused Booth to break his leg, as well as fragments of Lincoln's clothing snatched as he lay wounded in the theater.

On the eve of the centennial of Lincoln's death, Congress appropriated funds to restore Ford's

Theatre. The restoration, based upon Mathew Brady photographs taken the day Lincoln died, was so authentic it was decided that the building should be reopened as a theater. On Lincoln's Birthday, 1968, the first new production since *Our American Cousin* was staged in Ford's Theatre. A production of *A Christmas Carol* was first offered the following December.

So, after 103 years, the strange story of Ford's Theatre came full circle; audiences again watched actors play upon that stage; and audiences once again strained to see beyond the draperies into the shadows of that box just above and to the right of the apron. It is a fitting place for Dickens' tale of a past that haunts the present as well as the future.

In most American cities, the term
Christmas on the mall

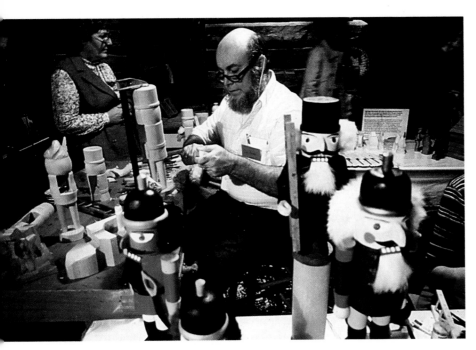

Craftspeople demonstrate the making of nutcrackers at the Smithsonian's National Museum of American History.

might be mistaken for Christmas *at* the mall, a term that conjures up images of scowling shoppers marching, bags in hand, under decorated fig trees to the beat of canned Christmas carols. Of course, Washington, like every major American city, has its suburbs, which like all suburbs, are served by shopping malls. But in Washington the "mall" is not a shopping center. The "mall" is the National Mall, a very broad alley of grass bordered by ordered rows of trees and lined on both sides by immense and grand public buildings. Officially, the National Mall is 14 blocks long. Unofficially, it stretches more than 23 blocks from the Capitol to the Lincoln Memorial and the Potomac River beyond. It is, unquestionably, one of the great urban spaces of the world.

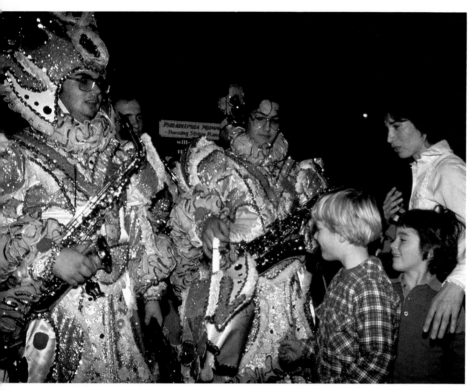

Mumming is demonstrated at The National Museum of American History during the Christmas season. Wildly costumed musicians and dancers play out dramas in which goodness triumphs over evil and the weak triumph over the strong. Christmas mumming certainly dates back to the Middle Ages and may descend from the Saturnalia, an ancient Roman festival celebrated, like Christmas, at midwinter.

The name *National Mall* offers a clue to the function of this immense space. It is a "national" place as opposed to a local one. If the city of Washington has such a thing as a "Main Street," it is Pennsylvania Avenue, not the Mall. On a local level, the National Mall is a kind of backyard, handsome and useful, but not exactly the center of things. It is a space that makes sense only as a symbol, a kind of national main street, central park, and cultural center rolled into one. Along its borders are the Capitol, the White House (via the Ellipse), and the nation's public record and vision of itself: the National Archives, the monuments and memorials to its national heroes, and the museums of the Smithsonian complex. (For a schematic

map of the National Mall, see the "Washington, D.C." article in *The World Book Encyclopedia.*)

When Pierre L'Enfant planned Washington, he included, where the Mall is now situated, a "Grand Avenue, 400 feet in breadth, and about a mile in length." He envisioned that it would be lined with "spacious houses and gardens, such as may accommodate foreign ministers." L'Enfant did not envision a national cultural center. The Mall as we know it today was not part of L'Enfant's original plan of Washington.

By 1848, when the cornerstone of the Washington Monument was laid, L'Enfant's plan for the city was considered dated and unimportant. By the early 1850's, his Grand Avenue had become overgrown in the fashion of the romantic school of English landscaping. It was at approximately this time that the word *mall* was first used to describe this space. The word is derived from the old French word *mail* or *maul*, which means mallet. A maul was used in the playing of the 17th-century game, pall-mall, pronounced pell mell, which can be loosely translated as ball mallet or hammer ball. The game consisted of hitting a ball through a circle at the end of a grassy alley. When the game went out of fashion, European cities were left with pall-mall alleys, which eventually became walkways, carriage drives, or bridle paths (the most famous of which was London's). Thus, in England, a grassy, shaded walk, or promenade, became known as a "mall." When English landscaping spread to America, English terminology spread with it.

The first step toward turning Washington's mall into a National Mall was unintentionally taken in 1855 when Congress authorized the construction of the Smithsonian Institution in that romantically overgrown park; the park also contained a singularly unhealthy swamp, the remnants of an old canal, and a railroad line and station. The "mall" remained in this condition until the early 20th century.

In 1893, millions of Americans visited the Columbian Exposition in Chicago, an early world's fair. What people saw and the images they took home changed the faces of cities and towns all over the country. The designers of the fair had, for the most part, been trained at the *École des Beaux-Arts* in Paris. They returned home to America imbued with ideals of the Beaux Arts. And on the lakefront in Chicago they erected the "white city," which to the majority of Americans who had never been to Europe looked like a vision of Imperial Rome. It was planned, ordered, fairly restrained, and grandiose in scale. People went home, looked around, and decided something was missing. Washingtonians, including con-

The Smithsonian Christmas tree display offers patrons the chance to see decorations from around the world as well as ornaments made by hand and from wholly natural materials. Each holiday season the tree display changes.

One of many Christmas trees at the National Museum of American History is displayed next to Horatio Greenough's statue of Washington in a Roman toga. Commissioned by Congress in the 1850's, the statue caused enormous trouble. Intended for the center of the Capitol rotunda, it was deemed inappropriate for that august spot, which has remained empty. It was eventually placed out on the west lawn. However, a half naked George Washington left out in the snow seemed to give everyone the shivers. The statue, which cost the then enormous sum of $45,000, was too valuable to destroy. So, Congress, long ago, sent the statue to the Smithsonian in the hope that it would quietly disappear.

gressmen, were no exception. They looked around, decided something was missing, and started a committee, which was peopled by the same artists and architects who planned the Chicago exposition. The result was, and is, modern-day Washington, including the National Mall—that symbolic main street of the nation.

Christmas on the Mall is, thus, more than Christmas in Washington. It is, like all events on the Mall, national, rather than local, in character—a symbol of how we view ourselves as a nation. Officially, the government of the United States does not celebrate Christmas. Unofficially, it does. The National Christmas Tree and the highly decorated White House testify to the fact. And up and down the length of the Mall stand the various publically funded museums that make up the Smithsonian complex; each sponsors holiday programs and exhibitions, which annually draw immense crowds from around the

nation and world. Although always a busy place, the Mall has, in fact, two big tourist seasons: summertime and Christmas.

Without the special programs, the Christmas decorations along the Mall would still draw tourists and Washingtonians. Both the National Christmas Tree and the Capitol Tree can be viewed from up and down and across the Mall's great vistas. The south facade of the White House, lighted for Christmas, can also be seen, via the Ellipse, from the unofficial, western section of the National Mall. Many of the Mall's public buildings are extravagantly decorated for the season; for example, the old Smithsonian Building, that fanciful, castlelike structure that sticks out onto the Mall, is usually festooned with evergreen garlands. The Library of Congress, which is just up Capitol Hill, has one of the city's most spectacular Christmas trees; often 30 feet tall, it takes a dozen members of the library grounds crew to tug and pull the monstrous tree through the 6-foot wide front doors. Adjacent to the Library of Congress is the Folger Shakespeare Library; the interior, which is English Renaissance in style, is decorated in historically appropriate fashion for the season. The Folger also offers "Yuletides of Yore" programs of Elizabethan prose, poetry, music, and "slapstick drama."

At the foot of Capitol Hill, at the east end of the Mall, is the conservatory of the U.S. Botanic Garden. (Funded by Congress, the Botanic Garden's collection began with plants brought to this country from China and Japan by Admiral Perry.) For the past 30 years, the conservatory has been the site of a Christmas greens exhibition, which transforms the east and west wings and connecting Orangery into a holiday fairyland. A recent exhibit was called "Home for Christmas" and featured 51 trees in the Orangery. The largest tree was "star spangled"; each of the 50 smaller trees was decorated to depict a song representing one of the states— for example, "My Old Kentucky Home" and "Back Home Again in Indiana." The five rooms in the west wing contained fireplace mantels and Christmas trees decorated to represent specific time periods: the mid-1880's and the mid-1940's, 50's, 70's, and 80's. The east wing, decorated especially for children, was dominated by a large "toyland" tree and miniature holiday landscapes and an old-fashioned sleigh. Evergreen wreaths and garlands are used every year to decorate the conservatory's interior and exte-

rior, including the exterior courtyards, where the Victorian lampposts are wound with evergreen roping. The Christmas greens exhibition closes around mid-December to make room for the equally spectacular poinsettia show, which is featured into the new year.

The majority of the buildings on the Mall are part of the Smithsonian Institution, which was founded when James Smithson, an English scientist, died in 1829. He left his entire estate— more than $500,000—to the United States with the instructions that an "establishment for the increase and diffusion of knowledge among men" be founded in his name. In the 159 years since Smithson's bequest, the Smithsonian has become the world's largest museum complex. At Christmas, the Smithsonian's various individual facilities offer an extraordinary variety of programs.

The National Museum of American History hosts the annual "Trees of Christmas" exhibit. On display are ten 8- to 12-foot trees, each decorated in a different theme or tradition by an artist in his or her own special medium. During one recent Christmas season, there was a *Christbaumschnitte* tree, trimmed with cut-paper designs and hand-sewn symbols in the German and Swiss tradition. Another tree was decorated with knotted cord and twine; square knots, half knots, and double half hitches formed macraméd bells, snowflakes, angels, and stars. A third tree was English Victorian. There

was a *Chrismon* tree trimmed with symbols from early Christian times and a "nature's bounty" tree decorated exclusively with natural materials—dried flowers and weeds, nuts, berries, as well as different varieties of feathers. An "American celebration" tree, which featured beaded and embroidered ornaments, symbolized the many ethnic backgrounds from which the people of the United States descend.

The Smithsonian's National Museum of American History also offers holiday workshops and classes on various subjects. Instructions in crafts have included the making of gingerbread houses, evergreen wreaths, paper angels,

and straw ornaments. A child-adult workshop has been offered in the Japanese art of origami, or paper folding. Participants learned to make a variety of holiday ornaments—for example, paper strawberries, stars, candy canes, and pandas.

In years past, the National Museum of American History has hosted holiday celebrations with jugglers, mimes, handbell ringers, barbershop quartets, Jewish instrumental music, Renaissance music and dance, movies, puppet shows, caroling, madrigal singers, and readings of holiday literature. Craftspeople throughout the museum demonstrate their art: the making of teddy bears; the carv-

At the foot of Capitol Hill is the Grant Memorial (insert), which in warm weather is reflected in an enormous pool. In winter, the pool becomes a skating rink. South of the Grant Memorial is the conservatory of the United States Botanic Garden, which offers two holiday exhibitions: the Christmas Greens display in early December; and the poinsettia show (left) from mid-December through the New Year.

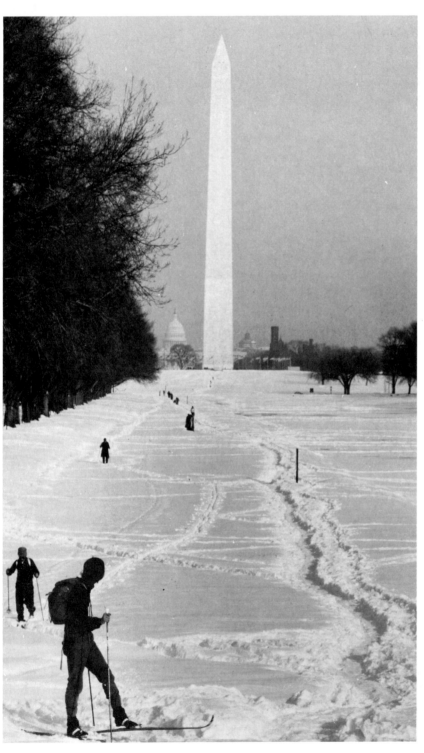

In winter the National Mall is used by skiers for both recreation and transportation. When snow snarls city traffic, office workers take to the Mall on skis.

ing of wooden nutcrackers; the baking of Jewish holiday cookies; the making of menorahs—the Jewish ceremonial candelabras; the fashioning of all kinds of holiday stars—Danish paper stars, Moravian Herrnhut stars, Polish stars, and even Filipino star lanterns. Utilizing its collection of antique presses, the museum also offers demonstrations of early printing techniques; at the end of the demonstration, audiences are presented with New Year's cards, which they have watched being printed.

The Smithsonian Institution also sponsors an architectural walking tour entitled "Christmas Around Lafayette Square." The event includes a discussion of and tour around the buildings and houses on Lafayette Square, a small rectangular park that George Washington set aside as a public space in 1791. Included on the tour is Blair House, the official government guest house, where President Truman lived during the last White House renovation; St. John's Church, called "the Church of the Presidents," which was built in 1816; the Dolley Madison House, from which the Widow Madison held sway over Washington society until her death in 1849; Decatur House, built by Commodore Stephen Decatur and lived in by both Henry Clay and Martin Van Buren (Decatur House, which has been meticulously restored, is open to the public.); the Tayloe-Cameron House, lived in by both the Civil War-era politician Senator Cameron of Pennsylvania and powerbroker Mark Hanna, who was called "the maker of presidents"; and, of course, the White House, which faces Lafayette Square on the south.

A number of office buildings face the square, as well as the Hay-Adams Hotel, which was erected on the site of the John Hay and Henry Adams houses. Here, Hay, personal secretary to Abraham Lincoln and secretary of state to Theodore Roosevelt, wrote his famous biography of Lincoln; and here Hay's good friend Henry Adams, grandson of John Quincy Adams and great-grandson of John Adams, wrote his histories and classic autobiography, *The Education of Henry Adams.*

The center of Lafayette Square is graced with an equestrian statue of Andrew Jackson, which was cast from bronze cannon captured by Jackson at the Battle of New Orleans. During the Christmas season the square and surrounding houses are charmingly decorated with historically appropriate wreaths and garlands.

Throughout the year, the National Museum of Natural History, next door to its American History counterpart, draws crowds of children with its permanent exhibits of reconstructed dinosaurs and animal dioramas. During the Christmas season, the museum produces puppet shows for its young patrons, including "The Beauty and the Beast," an annual favorite.

On the north side of the Mall between 3rd and 7th Streets is the august National Gallery of Art. At Christmas, evergreen wreaths on the two, 12-ton

For Christmas, the Library of Congress is decorated with an enormous tree in the ornate Main Entrance Hall. A crew of groundskeepers pull the tree through a 6-foot-wide door.

bronze doors mark the season; inside, banks of red poinsettias circle the Mercury-crowned, marble fountain in the center of the rotunda. But Christmas at the National Gallery is not a matter of decoration; here, the holiday is celebrated with art.

For families with children between the ages of 6 and 12, the National Gallery offers a program on holiday customs in other lands. This includes a lecture tour of the museum's collection related to Christmas. The National Gallery, which is affiliated with the Smithsonian, but governed by its own board of trustees, houses one of the finest collections of Western art in the world, including the only painting by Leonardo da Vinci outside Europe.

During the noon hour each week of the year, the National Gallery sponsors a program entitled "Painting of the Week," a 15-minute lecture and discussion on a single work from the collection. During December, the "painting of the week" is often one of the Gallery's many works related to Christmas; the collection contains Madonnas, Annunciations, and Nativity paintings by such artists as Giotto, Raphael, Botticelli, Verrocchio, Giorgione, Titian, van Eyck, and Rembrandt.

Christmas on the nation's "main street," like Christmas on Main Streets everywhere, includes holiday shopping. Both Washingtonians and tourists have found that the Mall is a good place to find unique gifts of superb quality. Many of the museums contain shops that offer gifts

unlike those available at department stores and shopping centers. The shop of the National Gallery, for example, carries Christmas cards that reproduce the many Nativity paintings from the collection. Beyond the Mall, the Folger Shakespeare Library shop sells Shakespearean T-shirts and cutout Elizabethan dollhouses. Scarves silk-screened with the ceiling pattern from the main reading room at the Library of Congress are available at the library's shop, where it is also possible to buy stencils with which to write messages in ancient Egyptian hieroglyphics.

One of the delights of Christmas on the Mall is the sight of ice skaters twirling around under the Capitol Tree. At the east end of the Mall is the Grant Memorial, which in the summer is reflected in an immense pool. In winter this pool often freezes over, offering residents and visitors a skating rink with a spectacular view down the full length of the Mall. A second pool in front of the National Archives, where rented skates are available, is also a favorite of skaters and sightseers. Both the Grant Memorial pool and the Archives pool, however, pale in comparison to the Reflecting Pool, which stretches 2,000 feet—nearly five blocks— from 17th Street to the foot of the Lincoln Memorial and which provides young skaters with an ideal race course.

The National Mall is also popular with skiers. When the city is hit with a severe snowstorm, cross-country skiers take to the nearly flat, two-mile long park for

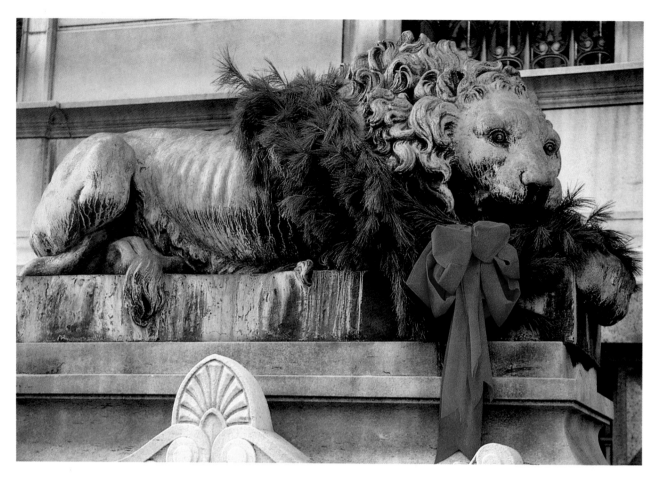

A bronze lion, cast from an original at St. Peter's in Rome, is dressed for Christmas at Washington's Corcoran Gallery of Art.

both recreation and transportation. Skiing up and down the Mall is an ideal way to move through the city when snow ties traffic into a snarl.

Although the National Mall brims over with Christmas shoppers and sightseers, its enormous length and breadth offers both breathing space in the center of a hectic city and places of quiet contemplation. Along the drives, the rows of graceful, winter-bare trees, frosted with ice and snow or even shrouded in Potomac fog, provide a scene of ethereal beauty. These trees, one of the nation's largest stands of the disease-prone American elm, are themselves something of a living museum, a beautiful, but sad reminder of what the streets of most American cities and towns have lost.

Under these trees, people stroll, summer and winter, past the Tidal Basin and the Jefferson Memorial, toward the templelike Lincoln Memorial, and beyond, north, to a more recent shrine—the black granite, Vietnam Veterans Memorial. Although this is the most visited site in Washington, it is a quiet place. Here, every day, including Christmas, silent pilgrims come to remember loved ones lost in that agonizing war. Wreaths are left along the wall, and cards are taped under the names of sons and daughters, spouses, and friends. The sight of those cards propped along the black, mirrorlike walls is a powerful image, a potent reminder of the meaning of the words *peace on earth.*

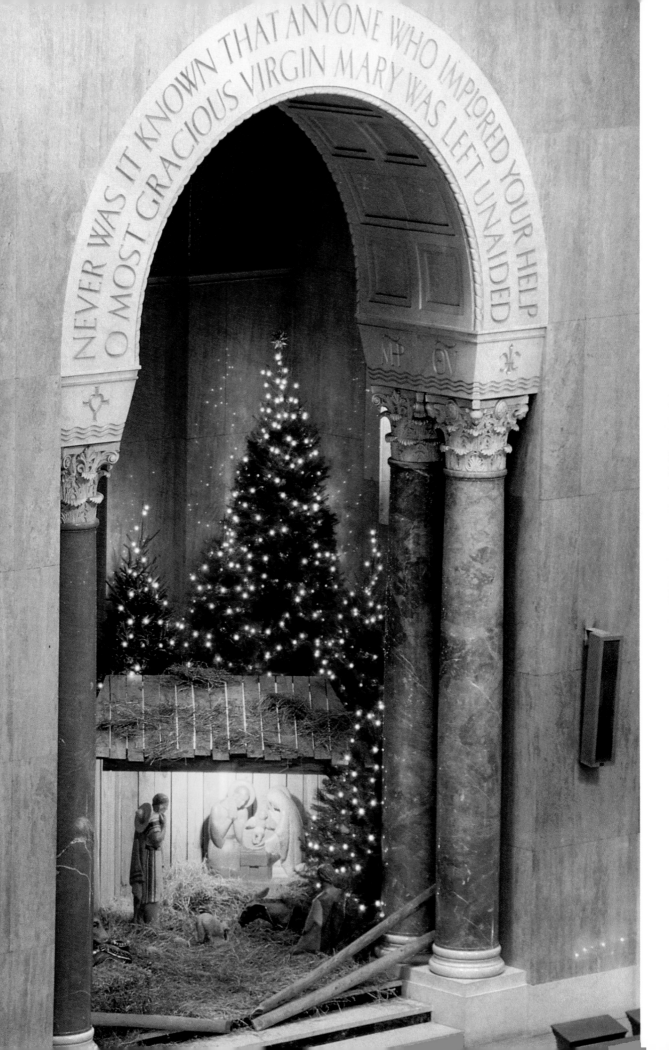

A Nativity scene is placed in a side chapel at the National Shrine of the Immaculate Conception, the nation's largest Roman Catholic church.

The word Advent *comes from the Latin word* adventus, *which means a coming or arrival.*

In suburban Kensington, Maryland, the grounds of the Mormon Temple, the only temple of that faith east of the Mississippi, are decorated for Christmas with thousands of miniature lights.

In Christian churches, the term Advent signifies the coming of the Christ child and is celebrated through the four weeks before Christmas. The Advent season, thus, begins on the Sunday nearest St. Andrew's Day, which is November 30, and continues until midnight, December 24, which marks the beginning of the Christmas season. In many churches, the Christmas season then continues until Epiphany, January 6, which in Western Christian churches is the day on which the coming of the Wise Men to the Christ child is celebrated.

In Washington, D.C., Advent and the twelve days of Christmas are celebrated in ways familiar to all Americans of the Christian faith. But as the nation's capital, Washington is a unique place. Institutions in the capital tend to be national, rather than local, in scope and intent. The churches of Washington are no exception. Most of the world's religions are represented in the city; Washington contains nearly 500 churches of 60 different faiths. They tend to be larger in scale than a city the size of Washington might warrant, and they tend to display a national, rather than local, out-

look. Unofficially, the nation's capital has become a world religious center.

Many Washington churches that are not identified as national institutions are locally associated with great historic traditions: the New York Avenue Presbyterian Church is known as "Lincoln's Church." The Civil War era pastor, Reverend Phineas D. Gurley, conducted Lincoln's funeral services. The present church, rebuilt in 1948, contains the original Lincoln pew.

St. John's Episcopal Church on Lafayette Square is known as the "Church of Presidents." In 1816 a committee was formed to "wait on the President of the United States (James Madison) and offer him a pew in this church, without his being obliged to purchase same." Madison chose Pew 54, but he payed the annual rental. Presidents Monroe, Adams, Jackson, Van Buren, and Harrison occupied Pew 54. It has since been set aside for presidents. In all, 10 presidents have occupied it, including Franklin D. Roosevelt.

St. Matthews Roman Catholic Cathedral, on Rhode Island Avenue, is associated with President Kennedy, who often attended Mass there. It was in St. Matthews that funeral services were held for him.

This combination of national interest and local history produces great traditions. These traditions are very apparent in the city's many Advent and Christmas worship services, which display great variety as well as signs of painstaking preparation. Of the many ecclesiastical services scheduled in Washington during Advent and the twelve days of Christmas, three programs stand out as being of national prominence: the midnight, Christmas Eve Mass at the National Shrine of the Immaculate Conception; the Advent and Christmas services at the Cathedral of SS. Peter and Paul, or the National Cathedral; and the Christmas Eve service at the Franciscan Monastery, which is affiliated with Washington's Catholic University of America.

The National Shrine of the Immaculate Conception, on the campus of the Catholic University of America, was designed to be "the greatest church edifice in the Western Hemisphere." It is the largest Catholic church in America. Generations of American Roman Catholics, as well as three popes, contributed to the building, which was begun in 1920. (Although opened in 1926, the Shrine is not yet fully completed.) The structure, Byzantine and Romanesque in style, is 465 feet in length and 238 feet across the sacristies; the dome, which rises 237 feet above the highest hill in the District of Columbia, can be seen from all sections of the city. At the National Shrine, Advent culminates at a midnight Mass on Christmas Eve, which is celebrated here as it has been every year since the crypt was opened for services in 1926. Roman Catholics from around the city and the nation arrive early on Christmas Eve to be assured a seat. For Christmas, the Shrine's interior, which is primarily alabaster ornamented with gold mosaics, is decorated with red flowers and evergreens; the red and green in contrast to the white and gold is spectacular. The midnight Mass is celebrated from the Mary Memorial Altar, a gift of Catholic women in America; this altar is a single block of golden onyx upon steps of white travertine marble. Both before and after the midnight Mass, celebrants pause for a moment of prayer and inspiration before the Shrine's Nativity scene, set in a side chapel, or before a reproduction in mosaic of Murillo's *Immaculate Conception*, which was given to the Shrine by Pope Benedict XV and Pope Pius XI. Christmas Eve Mass in this amazing church, which is indeed a national shrine, is an unforgettable experience.

The seat of the Protestant Episcopal Diocese of Washington— SS. Peter and Paul—is known as the Washington, or National, Cathedral. Unlike parish churches, the Cathedral has no regular membership. Its doors are open to everyone. While the Cathedral's own services conducted by the clergy of the Cathedral are Episcopal, special services are often held by various denominations, each according to its own traditions. Religious leaders of many different affiliations preach from the Cathedral's pulpit.

The National Cathedral is not supported by the Washington Diocese or by the Episcopal Church. It is being built and maintained by offerings and gifts from people of many different church affiliations. The Cathedral, by charter with the Congress of the United States, is legally obligated to function as a "House of Prayer for All People."

The National Cathedral, which was begun in 1907, is still under construction. Gothic in style, it is medieval in construction; that is, the Cathedral is being built exactly as Gothic cathedrals were built in the fourteenth century— entirely of stone worked by hand. While the nave is 100 feet from floor to ceiling vault, no steel was used in the building of walls or roofs. Exterior flying buttresses support the great height of the walls of the nave. Both the interior and exterior are richly carved

The Washington, or National, Cathedral is entirely constructed of stone cut by hand on Mount St. Alban—the site George Washington selected for a national house of prayer.

Christmas Eve Holy Communion before the altar at St. John's Church, the "Church of Presidents."

with figures that symbolize passages from the Old and New Testaments. Magnificent stained glass windows illustrate more Biblical stories: rose windows on the west, north, and south represent the *Seven Days of Creation,* the *Last Judgment,* and the *Church Triumphant.*

The story of the birth of Jesus Christ is told in stone and stained glass in the Cathedral's Bethlehem Chapel. The foundation stone of the Cathedral, which lies directly under the altar of the Bethlehem Chapel, was brought from the Shepherds' Field outside Bethlehem. The five stained glass windows of the ambulatory (the passage around the chapel altar) depict the genealogy of Christ, the appearance of the angels to the shepherds, the Annunciation, the Epiphany, and Simeon's acknowledgment of the Holy Child as the Christ.

Advent begins at the National Cathedral with Lessons and Carols on the fourth Sunday before Christmas. On an evening early in December, the doors of the Cathedral are opened to the public for a candlelight tour—a fascinating and appropriate way to visit a structure that is more of the fourteenth than the twentieth century. The tour concludes with holiday music, refreshments, and an opportunity for the tourist to catch a spectacular view of Washington by night from the Pilgrim Observatory Gallery.

Midway through Advent the Cathedral Choral Society performs their "Joy of Christmas" programs, which include the Advent wreath procession with Gregorian chant and handbells, a cantata, and familiar carols sung by the chorus and the audience. The Washington Cathedral Choir of Men and Boys sings Handel's *Messiah* in the Cathedral nave during Advent.

In preparation for Holy Communion at midnight on Christmas Eve, the Cathedral's Altar Guild begins decorating on the last Sunday of Advent. Usually, as many as 45 volunteers complete the work in 2 to 3 days. The high altar, constructed of 12 stones from Solomon's quarry in Jerusalem, is for Christmas banked with more than 400 poinsettias. Many pounds of boxwood, Douglas fir, holly, as well as magnolia grown locally are used to decorate throughout the Cathedral. Lighted evergreen trees and wreaths twinkle from the shadows of the many chapels.

The magnificent architecture, the superb craftsmanship shown in the construction, the lavish and handsome decorations, and the very real ecumenical spirit make Holy Communion on Christmas Eve in the National Cathedral a memorable experience. Cathedral worship services continue on Christmas Day; normally one is nationally televised. The Cathedral remains decorated through Epiphany, January 6. The public is, of course, welcome to attend services and programs or to simply tour the buildings and gardens.

During some Christmas seasons, the Cathedral gardens are the center of a great deal of attention. The focus is a thorn tree planted in 1900 by the first Episcopal bishop of Washington, Henry Yates Satterlee. While visiting England, Bishop Satterlee was given a slip from the famous Glastonbury Thorn. By tradition, the Glastonbury Thorn sprang from Joseph of Arimathea's staff, which was said to have been cut from the same tree that supplied the crown of thorns. (Joseph of Arimathea, who offered his tomb for the burial of Christ, is believed to have introduced Christianity into Britain.) The original thorn tree was destroyed by Oliver Cromwell's soldiers during the English civil war, but cuttings of it had already been planted elsewhere. Legend aside, the Glastonbury Thorn blooms both summer and winter. The second bloom usually comes at Christmas—in honor, it is said, of the birth of Jesus.

Bishop Satterlee's slip, which he planted on the grounds of the new cathedral being constructed in Washington, first bloomed on Christmas in 1918. It continues, irregularly, to do so to this day.

On Christmas Eve, Christians of all denominations gather at Washington's Franciscan Monastery Memorial Church of the Holy Land. Here are facsimiles of the Chief Shrines of the Christian religion: the Garden of Gethsemane, the Holy Sepulchre, the Catacombs of Rome, and the Grotto of Bethlehem. The Franciscan Monastery's Grotto of Bethlehem is a faithful reproduction of the Grotto of the Nativity in Bethlehem. At exactly the hour at which the Christmas Eve service is held in Bethlehem an identical service is held in Washington. When the Christmas Eve Mass is completed, a procession headed by a cross bearer winds its way through the Monastery Church. With great care, one of the celebrants carries a life-sized wooden image of the Infant. (The image was carved in Barcelona, Spain. Before it was removed to Washington, the image was taken to Bethlehem, where it was placed on the silver star that is identified as the spot where Jesus was born.) Descending a spiral staircase, the procession reaches the crypt. The altar stands between two flights of stairs. Below the altar is a facsimile of the silver star that in Bethlehem marks the spot where Jesus was born. Upon arriving in the grotto the deacon chants the gospel of the first Mass of Christmas. With the words "and she brought forth her first-born son," the wooden image of the Infant is placed upon the star, which bears the inscription, in Latin, "Here Jesus Christ was born of the Virgin Mary." When the deacon reads "and wrapped him in swaddling clothes," the image is raised from the star and carried to the Place of the Manger, which is two steps below and to the right of the star. The ceremony concludes when the image of the Baby Jesus is layed into the straw arranged in the manger. The long procession of celebrants climbs up the stairs, winds its way through the church, and out into the night. It is Christmas morning. The Christ is born.

A National Cathedral Christmas service for children includes a living Nativity scene in the Bethlehem Chapel. Below this chapel is the Cathedral cornerstone, which is made of stones collected from the Shepherd's Field outside of Bethlehem.

Home for Christmas

Although Washington has its share of government officials who flee the town at Christmastime, the city is not as transient as many believe it to be. Washington families gather together at this season to attend church, to share Christmas dinner, to exchange gifts, to enjoy the beauty of the often snow-clad city, and to reminisce about former Christmases in this historic town.

Few have been around long enough to recall the very old sights and sounds of Christmases past, but they have heard stories of Christmas in old Washington. One hundred years ago, most

In the 1980's, fashionable Washingtonians Christmas shop in such lavishly decorated malls as Georgetown's Victorian Arcade (left). In the 1880's, the fashionable, including presidents and first ladies, shopped late—Christmas Eve—along Pennsylvania Avenue.

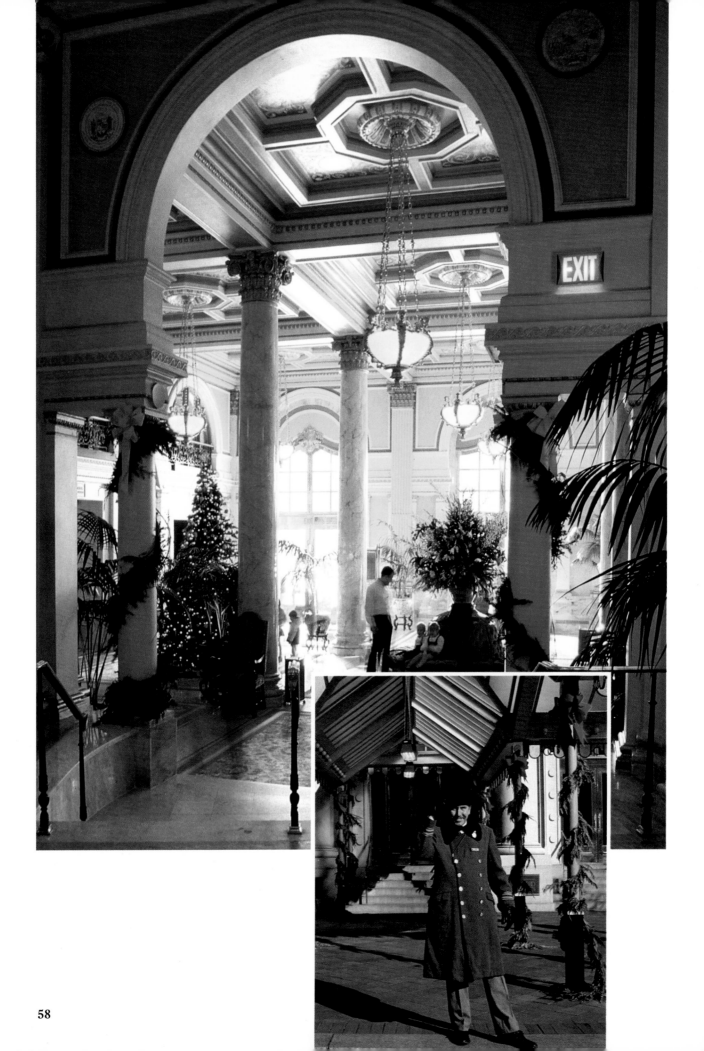

Washington's venerable Willard Hotel is decorated for the holidays exactly as it was in its heyday as the city's center of political intrigue. Lincoln was smuggled into the Willard before his inauguration; Julia Ward Howe wrote "The Battle Hymn of the Republic" during a stay at the hotel.

families made a trip to the Centre Market on 7th Street and Pennsylvania Avenue, where the National Archives now stands, to purchase a Christmas tree and greenery. During Christmas week, farmers came to the market with wagons full of evergreen, holly, mistletoe, and laurel. At that time, every church and home was draped with greens for the holidays. Some said greenery was more plentiful than meat and vegetables. But the stalls inside the market also sold the food necessary for an ample Christmas dinner— vegetables, hams and turkeys, fruits and nuts. Today, the Eastern Market near Capitol Hill stands as the last example of this old Washington tradition.

Washingtonians, like most Americans, do their Christmas shopping in multileveled, shopping malls, such as Georgetown Park with its Victorian arcade shops, green wrought iron and shining brass trim, and skylit atrium. Georgetown Park is always lavishly decorated for Christmas and provides costumed musicians and carolers to entertain shoppers. Although some Washingtonians remain loyal to the now often deserted downtown department stores, the days of bustling open-air Christmas shopping, where once even the nation's president could be seen selecting Christmas gifts, are nearly over.

President Abraham Lincoln often visited a toy shop that stood near 12th Street and New York Avenue. There he bought toy soldiers for his sons. President Taft enjoyed shopping on Pennsylvania Avenue. He would go on foot accompanied by an aide, and both would return long after dark laden with bundles. President Warren G. Harding often made Christmas purchases for friends in a Washington bookstore. Not wanting to be noticed, he went late, walked briskly, wore a dark coat, and pulled his hat down low.

For good or for bad, many old Washington Christmas traditions have disappeared forever: the firecrackers, pistol shots, and general rowdiness of Christmas Eve celebrations; the wartime Christmases when Washington families took servicemen into their homes for dinner; and the sight of Santa, his pack on his back, arriving at the Navy Yard on Christmas morning to distribute packages to each house in the long row of quarters as the sound of the Navy Band playing carols drifted up and down the street.

But Washington remembers, in its own way, Yuletides of long ago. The long-time residents of the city still keep old traditions. Some take a Christmas candlelight tour of Old Town Alexandria, George Washington's hometown, and enjoy music and refreshments in historic homes. Others spend time during the holidays at Washington's Rock Creek Park, where they join the miller and hear folk tales told around the old pot-belly stove. Others delight in the history of the Willard Hotel, the center of Washington politics in mid-nineteenth century, now a restored landmark, which is beautifully decorated for the holidays.

Christmas Eve at home. After church, Santa's gifts are opened.

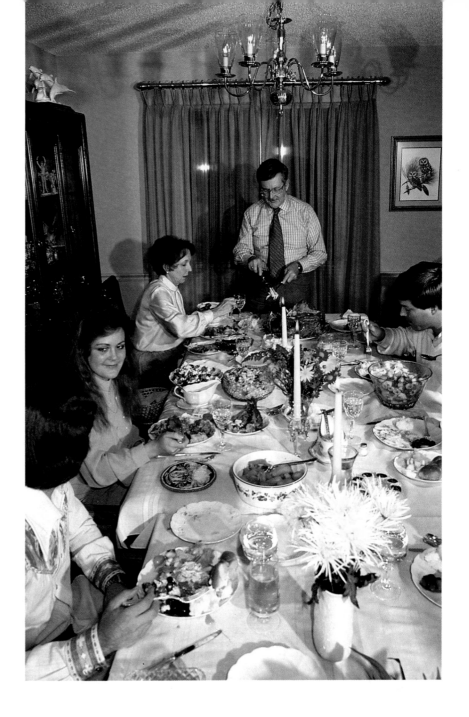

A Washington family has dinner on Christmas afternoon.

As the season comes to a close, the citizens of Washington prepare for the last of the holiday celebrations—the ringing in of the new year. At the Kennedy Center, Washingtonians, dressed in ball gowns and tuxedoes, waltz through New Year's Eve in the Center's Grand Foyer. A far less formal celebration takes place at the historic Old Post Office Pavilion. As a giant stamp is lowered from the Pavilion clock, timed to reach

In Washington, the New Year is celebrated before the old Post Office building, where a stamp is dropped down the tower at the stroke of midnight.

the base of the old post office tower precisely at midnight, much of Washington celebrates the end of one year and the beginning of another. Another year to add to history in a city where the making of history never stops.

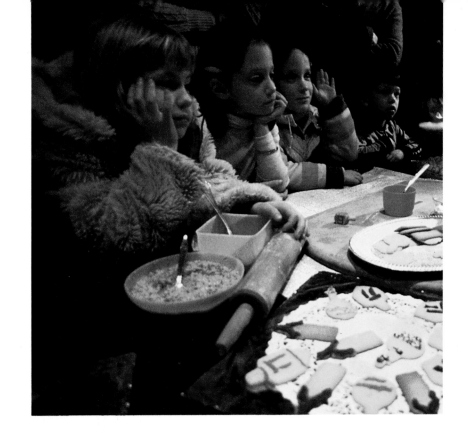

Cookie baking is demonstrated at the Smithsonian's National Museum of American History (right). A gingerbread house, made by a White House chef, is on display in the State Dining Room.

Crafts

Stencil Patterns

Cut along these lines.

Cut along these lines.

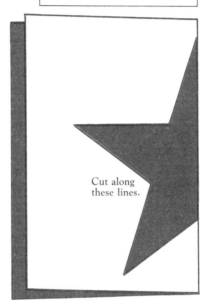

Cut along these lines.

To make the bell, tree, and star stencils:

(1) Trace patterns on tracing paper and cut them out.

(2) Cut construction paper into 4-inch by 3-inch pieces, and fold into 2-inch by 3-inch pieces.

(3) Place one of the patterns on a piece of folded construction paper, lining up the right side of the pattern with the fold in the paper. Outline the pattern onto the construction paper.

(4) Cut along the lines you traced and unfold the paper. You now have a stencil.

Point A

To make the snowflake stencil:

(1) Trace the pattern on tracing paper and cut out the darkened sections.

Point A

(2) Cut a piece of construction paper 5 inches square. Mark its center with a small circle. As you fold the square, keep the circle visible.

(3) Fold the square in half, then in half again, and then into a triangle, along the fold line extending from the circle.

(4) Place the tracing paper over the folded construction paper, lining up the circle with point A on the pattern, and trace the darkened sections.

(5) Cut out those sections and unfold the construction paper. You now have a stencil, as pictured in the inset to the left.

To make Christmas wrapping paper:

(1) Lightly tape stencil to tissue paper.

(2) Dip sponge into water-thinned poster paint and pat open area of stencil.

(3) Repeat with same or different stencil to complete wrapping paper.

Uncle Sam Ornament

Material list:
- cardboard tube from toilet paper roll
- bond paper
- crayons or markers
- pencil
- tape
- glue (preferably a stick glue)
- string or yarn
- snub-nosed scissors

(3) Trace pattern B on bond paper, and color one side blue. Cut out the pattern. If the marker has bled through, trace another pattern B, cut it out, and glue it to the white side of the first pattern.

(4) Using the pencil, poke a hole through the black dot in the center of the hat brim. Then, cut carefully along the lines, radiating from the center.

(1) Trace pattern A on bond paper, and color with markers or crayons as shown in the pattern.

(2) Trim the excess bond paper and glue the pattern onto the cardboard tube, the white and red stripes being parallel to the length of the tube.

Pattern A

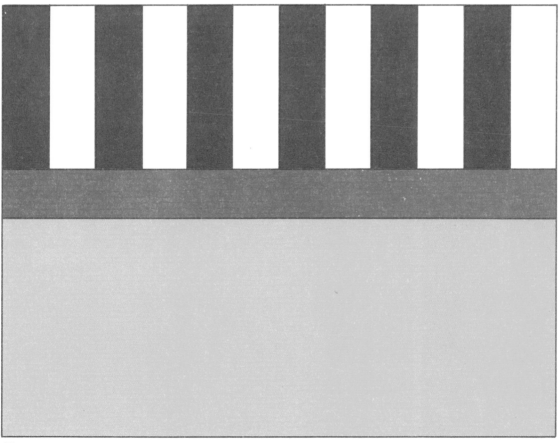

(5) Place the cardboard tube on the table, pink side up. Spread a little glue around the pink part of the tube, just above the blue stripe. Holding the hat brim (white side up) over the tube, push the tube up through the center of the hat brim until the blue stripe on the tube meets the hat brim.

(6) Trace pattern C on bond paper, and cut it out, also carefully cutting along the parallel lines. Glue the beard one-half inch from the bottom of the pink area.

(7) Trace patterns D, E, and F. Color the nose pink, the berry red, and the leaf green. Cut them out. Place glue only on the top of the nose and attach it halfway between the white beard and the hat brim. Glue the berry to the leaf and attach to the hat as shown in the illustration.

(8) With a black marker, draw in the eyes and mouth as shown in the illustration.

(9) Poke a hole near the top of the hat for the yarn or string. Tie and hang up.

Pattern B

Pattern D

Pattern E

Pattern F

Pattern C

Christmas Star Mobile

Material list:
- pencil
- cardboard
- tracing paper
- snub-nosed scissors
- straight pins
- white and green yarn
- tape
- hair spray or spray starch
- thread
- drinking straws, cut into three 3-inch lengths
- heavy cardboard

(1) Cut tracing paper and cardboard into 3-inch squares.

(2) Trace the star and Christmas tree patterns (figures 1 & 2) onto the tracing paper and tape each to a square of cardboard. Insert pins, as in figures 3 & 4.

(3) Cut an 18-inch piece of white yarn for the star, green for the tree.

(4) Wrap the yarn in and out of the pins as in figures 3 & 4. Tape the ends to the edge of the cardboard.

(5) Spray the yarn until soaked with hair spray or spray starch. Let dry completely.

Figure 1

Figure 3

Figure 2

Figure 4

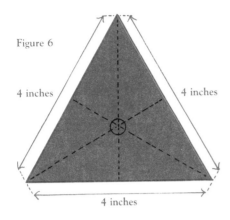

Figure 6

4 inches

4 inches

4 inches

(10) Cut a triangle, 4 inches on each side, out of the heavy cardboard, as in figure 6. Make a hole at each of the corners and in the center. Attach a string to the center.

(11) Tie a different length of string to the center of each straw. Tie the other end of the string to one of the triangle's corners. You can now hang up your mobile.

(6) Untape and remove the star and tree. Trim the ends of the yarn.

(7) Make 2 more stars and 2 more trees.

(8) Tie different lengths of string to the tops of each ornament.

(9) Attach an ornament to each end of the 3 straws, as in figure 5.

Figure 5

3 inches

Garland Paper Chain

Material list:
- red paper, white paper, blue paper
- glue
- pencil
- snub-nosed scissors
- tape

(1) Cut the paper into strips ½″ by 5½″.

(2) Take both ends of a paper strip and join them together with glue.

(3) Take another strip of paper; put it through the first ring; and join both ends together with glue.

(4) The rings can be strung together in repetition of a regular color pattern, in random color patterns, or in a garland all of one color. Continue adding strips of paper until you have reached the length you desire.

(5) Different lengths of garland can be taped to a door or wall in the form of a Christmas tree. Cut out the tree base from blue paper, and the star from white paper, using the patterns and dimensions below. Use red paper for the candles, and yellow for the flames, following the pattern and dimensions below. Arrange the pieces as in the illustration below, and tape to the door or wall.

(6) Garlands can also be suspended from a chandelier to the edges of the ceiling.

(7) Long garlands can be used to decorate a Christmas tree.

Christmas Door Decoration

Material list:
- thick color paper
- snub-nosed scissors
- needle and thread
- tracing paper or thin bond paper
- tape
- pencil
- red or green ribbon bow

(1) Trace each of the patterns below onto separate pieces of tracing paper or thin bond paper. Cut them out.

(2) Cut out 2 pieces of the thick color paper, 3″ by 4″. Fold them in half along the 4″ length. Tape each pattern onto a piece of the folded paper, lining up the right edge of the pattern with the fold in the color paper.

(3) Cut along each of the solid, parallel lines; then along the outlines of the tree and bell. Open them out flat.

(4) On a piece of the color paper, draw a stem and a clapper, each about 3″ long. Follow the shapes pictured here. Cut them out.

(5) Weave the stem up the center of the tree, in and out of the slits. Do the same with the clapper. Then twist the stem and clapper 90 degrees, so that the tree and bell "open up." Using the needle, loop a piece of thread through their tops.

(6) Make as many ornaments as you need for the ribbon bow. Then attach them to the bow, as shown above.

Recipes
from the White House

Mrs. Lyndon B. Johnson's POPOVERS

1 c. sifted all-purpose flour
¼ t. salt
2 eggs, beaten
1 c. milk
2 tbs. shortening, melted

Combine flour and salt in a bowl. Blend together last 3 ingredients. Gradually add these to the dry ingredients, beating constantly about 1 minute, or until batter is smooth. Fill greased sizzling-hot pans ¾ full and bake at 450° F. 20 minutes. Reduce heat to 350° F. and continue baking 15 to 20 minutes, or until deep golden brown.

8 medium popovers

Andrew Jackson's SPOON BREAD

1 c. white hominy grits or water-ground white corn meal
1½ t. salt
1 c. cold water
2 c. hot milk
2 eggs, beaten
3 tbs. butter or margarine

Stir together first 3 ingredients until smooth. Blend in hot milk. Cook and stir over low heat until mixture begins to thicken. Remove from heat. Blend in eggs and butter. Turn into a well-greased 1-quart casserole. Bake at 350° F. 45 minutes, or until firm to the touch. Serve with a spoon from the casserole with plenty of butter or margarine.

About 6 servings

Martha Washington's SPICED GYNGERBREDE

2¾ c. sifted all-purpose flour
1 t. baking soda
½ t. salt
2 t. ground ginger
1 t. ground cinnamon
1 t. ground mace
1 t. ground nutmeg
½ c. hydrogenated shortening
2 tbs. grated orange peel
½ c. packed brown sugar
3 eggs
¼ c. strained orange juice
¼ c. brandy
1 c. molasses

Sift the first 7 ingredients together and set aside. Thoroughly blend together the next 3 ingredients. Add eggs, one at a time, beating until light and fluffy after each addition. Mix heated orange juice and brandy with molasses. Alternately, add dry ingredients and molasses mixture to creamed mixture, beginning and ending with dry ingredients. After each addition, beat until blended. Turn batter into greased 9x9x2-inch baking pan. Bake at 350° F. 30 to 40 minutes. Let cool.

One 9-inch square gingerbread

Recipes used with permission of *The Culinary Arts Institute's The Presidents' Own White House Cookbook* © 1975 Delair Publishing Company.

ROAST LAMB WITH ELDERBERRY SAUCE

5 to 7-pound leg of lamb (boned)
3 c. crumbled corn bread
¼ c. minced parsley
½ t. salt
pinch of pepper
3 tbs. mint sauce
1 egg, beaten
¼ c. milk
elderberry sauce (see recipe below)

Toss together all the ingredients from corn bread to milk. Place this stuffing into the cavity left by deboning the leg of lamb. Fasten the opening and place lamb on a rack in a shallow roasting pan. Roast 35 minutes to the pound in a 300°–325° F. oven. When ready to serve, slice lamb and pour elderberry sauce over the slices.

6 to 8 servings

ELDERBERRY SAUCE

2 tbs. pan drippings
1½ tbs. flour
½ t. dry mustard
½ c. Burgundy
½ c. elderberry jelly
1 tbs. mixed grated orange
    and lemon peel

Stir dry mustard into a roux of pan drippings and flour. Gradually add wine, stirring constantly. Bring to boiling. Cook and stir 1 to 2 minutes. Add jelly and citrus peel. Heat and stir until jelly is melted and sauce is smooth.

About 1 cup sauce

Andrew Jackson's TURKEY HASH

medium-sized turkey (8 to 10 pounds)
celery
onion
1 bay leaf
salt
2 pods of red pepper
4 tbs. butter
2 tbs. flour
Worcestershire sauce
white pepper

Prepare turkey for a roaster. Add sufficient water to make stock. Put in next 5 ingredients. Cover; allow to cook slowly until tender. Do not brown. Pour off and strain stock; allow to cool. When fat rises to top, skim off and discard. When turkey has cooled, pull apart, discarding all skin, bones, and gristle. Cut in large, bite-size pieces. Make a roux of the butter and flour in a large skillet or saucepan. Heat until bubbly. Stirring constantly, add gradually a quart of the turkey stock. Bring to boiling and cook 1 to 2 minutes. Season with Worcestershire sauce. To each quart of sauce, add 2 quarts of cut-up turkey. Add white pepper, if needed, and serve very hot.

8 to 10 servings

Teddy Roosevelt's CHRISTMAS TURKEY

18-pound turkey
1 dozen large oysters, minced very fine
2 c. fine bread crumbs
1 tbs. chopped herbs (parsley, thyme,
    or sweet marjoram)
    salt
    pepper

Prepare turkey for roasting. Combine the rest of the ingredients. Salt and pepper to taste. Stuff turkey and roast.

PHEASANTS WITH SPAETZLE

2 pheasants, cleaned and quartered
2 qt. boiling water
4 chicken bouillon cubes
½ c. flour
1 c. butter
1 t. paprika
7 tbs. flour
1 c. Chablis
1 c. dairy sour cream

Put necks, backs, giblets, etc. of pheasants and bouillon cubes into water. Cook until stock is reduced to 1½ quarts. Flour remaining pieces of pheasant. Saute in ½ cup butter until brown, and reserve. In large frying pan, melt ½ cup butter, add paprika and all but 1 cup of strained pheasant stock. Bring to boiling. Gradually stir in remaining stock and 7 tbs. flour. Boil 1 to 2 minutes. Stir in Chablis and cook gently 30 minutes. Add pheasant; cover and cook 1 to 1½ hours. Remove pheasant. Stir in sour cream, about a spoonful at a time, with gentle heating. Place pheasant in serving dish, spaetzle in a bowl. Over each, spoon some of the paprika sauce.

About 6 servings

SPAETZLE

3 eggs, beaten
½ t. salt
1 c. heavy cream
2 c. flour
chicken stock
¼ c. butter

Combine first 3 ingredients. Stir in flour to make a stiff batter. Dip a teaspoon into batter, just enough to cover the end of it. From end of teaspoon, drop batter into boiling chicken stock. Cook 5 minutes. Drain and saute in butter until light brown.

WILD RICE CASSEROLE

½ c. wild rice, soaked overnight
½ c. brown rice, soaked overnight
1 c. sliced fresh mushrooms
½ c. chopped white onion
½ c. shredded sharp cheddar cheese
6 tbs. cooking oil
1 c. hot chicken broth
2 tbs. sherry
salt and pepper
pimento strips

Drain rice, and combine with next 3 ingredients. Place in 1½-quart casserole or 8x8x2-inch baking dish. Stir in next 3 ingredients. Sprinkle with salt and pepper. Garnish with pimento strips. Bake at 350° F. 1 hour.

6 to 8 servings

Dolley Madison's FRYING HERBS

1½ pounds fresh spinach
½ c. chopped parsley
6 green onions
salt to taste
butter

Wash and drain spinach leaves and parsley. Chop parsley and onions. Combine all 3 ingredients in a pan with a bit of butter the size of a walnut and some salt. Cook over low heat, covered, until done. Serve with slices of broiled calf's liver, small rashers of bacon, and fried eggs—the latter on the herbs, the other in a separate dish.

About 4 servings

CUMIN-FLAVORED SPRING PEAS

½ t. cumin seed
¼ c. water
2 lb. fresh peas
¼ c. butter
6 green onions, chopped
½ c. heavy cream

Soak cumin seed in the water. Shell peas. One pound of peas unhulled is about 1 cup of young peas hulled. Saute onions in saucepan with butter until transparent, but not browned. Add cumin seed, water, and then peas. Add more water, if necessary. Cover and cook slowly until almost done, about 10–20 minutes. Add heavy cream; heat thoroughly; but do not boil.

4 servings

Martha Washington's FRUITED WHITE CAKE

1 c. butter
1 c. sugar
5 eggs, separated
2½ c. sifted all-purpose flour
1 t. ground mace
¼ t. ground nutmeg
1 c. diced assorted candied fruits
2 tbs. red wine
2 t. brandy

Cream butter. Beat in sugar gradually. Add egg yolks, one at a time, beating until fluffy after each addition. Sift spices with flour and combine with fruit. Combine everything and mix well. Blend in wine and brandy. Fold in egg whites, beaten until stiff, not dry, peaks are formed. Turn into greased (bottom only) and lightly floured 9-inch tube pan. Bake at 325° F. about 1¼ hours. Place pan on rack and let cool completely. Frosting may be used.

One 9-inch tubed fruit cake

Mrs. Harry Truman's OZARK PUDDING

1 egg
¾ c. sugar
¼ c. all-purpose flour
1¼ t. baking powder
⅛ t. salt
½ c. chopped nuts
½ c. chopped apple
1 t. vanilla extract

Beat together egg and sugar until thoroughly blended and smooth. Blend next 3 ingredients and mix into egg-sugar mixture. Stir in final ingredients. Turn into greased 8-inch pie pan. Bake at 350° F. about 35 minutes. Serve warm or cold with whipped cream or ice cream.

6 servings

Teddy Roosevelt's PHILADELPHIA SAND TARTS

1 c. butter
2 t. vanilla extract
2 c. sugar
2 eggs
1 egg, separated
4 c. sifted all-purpose flour
   sugar and cinnamon

Cream butter and vanilla extract. Add sugar gradually, beating constantly until light and fluffy. Add eggs, one at a time, beating well after each addition. Beat in egg yolk, then blend in flour. Mix well. Chill, if necessary. Roll thin on lightly floured surface, cut with round cookie cutter 2½ inches in diameter. Brush with remaining egg white, slightly beaten. Sprinkle with sugar and cinnamon. Place on greased cookie sheets and bake at 350° F. 8 to 10 minutes.

About 6 dozen cookies

PLANTATION POUND CAKE

1 lb. butter
½ t. lemon extract
½ t. freshly grated nutmeg
10 eggs, separated
1 lb. confectioners' sugar, sifted
1 lb. all-purpose flour, sifted (4c.)
1 tbs. French brandy

Cream first 3 ingredients until soft as thick cream. Beat egg yolks until thick. Alternate mixing sugar, flour, and egg yolks into creamed butter. Beat well. Mix in brandy. Gently fold in well-beaten egg whites until well-blended. Grease and dust with flour 10-inch tubed pan or two 9x5x3-inch loaf pans. Pour in batter and bake at 350° F. about 1 hour and 45 minutes.

One 10-inch tubed cake or 2 loaves

Mrs. Theodore Roosevelt's INDIAN PUDDING

3 c. milk
½ c. yellow corn meal
¼ c. sugar
1 t. salt
1 t. ground cinnamon
½ t. ground ginger
1 egg, well beaten
½ c. light molasses
2 tbs. butter
1 c. cold milk

Scald 3 c. milk in a double boiler. Stirring constantly, blend scalded milk into a mixture of the next 5 ingredients. Vigorously stir some of this mixture into a blend of beaten egg and molasses. Stir this blend into hot corn meal mixture. Stirring constantly, cook over boiling water until very thick (about 10 minutes). Beat in butter. Turn into buttered 1½-qt. casserole. Pour cold milk over top. Bake at 300° F. for 2 hours, or until browned. Serve warm with heavy cream or ice cream.

About 6 servings

While Shepherds Watched Their Flocks

Favorite Carol of George Washington

Nahum Tate, 1652–1715

Arranged from George F. Handel, 1685–1759

Allegro moderato

1. While shep-herds watched their flocks by night, All seat-ed on the ground, The an-gel of the Lord came down, And glo-ry shone a - round, And glo-ry shone a - round.
2. "Fear not!" said he for might-y dread Had seized their trou-bled mind, "Glad tid-ings of great joy I bring, To you and all man-kind, To you and all man-kind.
3. "To you, in Da-vid's town this day, Is born of Da-vid's line, The Sav-ior who is Christ the Lord; And this shall be the sign, And this shall be the sign:
4. "The heaven-ly Babe you there shall find To hu-man view dis-played, All mean-ly wrapped in swath-ing bands, And in a man-ger laid, And in a man-ger laid."

From *The International Book of Carols* edited by Walter Ehret and George K. Evans. Copyright © 1963, 1980 by Walter Ehret and George K. Evans. Reprinted by permission of the Stephen Greene Press, a wholly owned subsidiary of Viking Penguin Inc.

We Three Kings of Orient Are

*Favorite Carol of
Abraham Lincoln*

John H. Hopkins, 1857

John H. Hopkins, 1857

Moderato

1. We three kings of O - ri - ent are; Bear - ing
2. Born a King on Beth - le - hem's plain, Gold I
3. Frank - in - cense to of - fer have I, In - cense
4. Myrrh is mine, its bit - ter per - fume Breathes a
5. Glo - rious now be - hold Him a - rise, King and

gifts, we trav - erse a - far Field and foun - tain,
bring, to crown Him a - gain, King for - ev - er
owns a De - i - ty nigh. Pray'r and prais - ing
life of gath - er - ing gloom; Sor - r'wing, sigh - ing,
God and Sac - ri - fice, Al - le - lu - ia,

moor and moun - tain, Fol - low - ing yon - der star.
ceas - ing nev - er O - ver us all to reign.
all men rais - ing, Wor - ship Him, God most high.
bleed - ing, dy - ing, Sealed in the stone cold tomb.
Al - le - lu - ia, Earth to the heav'ns re - plies.

REFRAIN

O— star of won - der, star of night, Star with roy - al beau - ty bright,

West - ward lead - ing still pro - ceed - ing, Guide us to Thy per - fect light.

O Come, All Ye Faithful

Favorite Carol of Dwight D. Eisenhower

J.F. Wade
Translation: Frederick Oakley, alt. 1841

J.F. Wade, ca 1740

2. *Cantet nunc Io! chorus angelorum;*
   Cantet nunc aula caelestium:
   Gloria, gloria, in excelsis Deo:
   Venite adoremus, etc.

2. Sing, choirs of angels, sing in exultation,
   Sing, all ye citizens of heav'n above!
   Glory to God, all glory in the highest!
   O come, let us adore Him, etc.

3. *Ergo qui natus die hodierna,*
   Jesu, tibi sit gloria!
   Patris aeterni Verbum caro factum:
   Venite adoremus, etc.

3. Yea, Lord, we greet Thee, born this holy
   morning,
   Jesus, to Thee be glory giv'n!
   Word of the Father, now in flesh
   appearing:
   O come, let us adore Him, etc.

Acknowledgments

Cover: © Jack Novak, Photri from Marilyn Gartman
2: © John Aikins, Uniphoto
6: © Lani Howe, Photri
7: © Everett C. Johnson from Marilyn Gartman
8: © Uniphoto
9: © Steven Gottlieb, FPG
10: (*Left*) © John Aikins, Uniphoto
(*Right*) © A. Pierce Bounds, Uniphoto
11: © Rick Brady, Uniphoto
12: Franklin D. Roosevelt Library
13: © Lani Howe, Photri
15: © Everett C. Johnson from Marilyn Gartman
16: © Richard Howard, Black Star
18: The White House
19: The White House
20: The White House
21: (*Top*) The White House
(*Bottom*) UPI/Bettmann Newsphotos
22: The White House
23: The White House
24: The Newberry Library, Chicago
25: © John Ficara, Woodfin Camp, Inc.
26: The Newberry Library, Chicago
27: (*Bottom*) The Newberry Library, Chicago
(*Top*) © John Aikins, Uniphoto
28: UPI/Bettmann Newsphotos
29: Bettmann Archive
30: Harry S. Truman Library
31: (*Top*) Dwight D. Eisenhower Library
(*Bottom*) National Museum of American History
32: (*Left*) © Brad Markel
(*Right*) John F. Kennedy Library

34: © Fred J. Maroon
35: © Robert M. Anderson, Uniphoto
36: © Lisa Berg
37: © Joan Marcus
38: © Joan Marcus
39: National Museum of American History
40: National Museum of American History
41: National Museum of American History
42: National Museum of American History
44: (*Left*) Everett C. Johnson from Marilyn Gartman
(*Right*) © Bill Weems, Woodfin Camp, Inc.
46: © Dennis Brack, Black Star
47: Library of Congress
49: © Ron Goor, Bruce Coleman Inc.
50: The Shrine of the Immaculate Conception
51: © Everett C. Johnson from Marilyn Gartman
53: © Fred J. Maroon
54: St. John's Church
55: © Mark Broffman
56: © Ron Goor, Bruce Coleman Inc.
57: The Newberry Library, Chicago
58: (*Top*) © Carol Highsmith
(*Bottom*) © Carol Highsmith
60: © Dennis Brack, Black Star
61: (*Left*) © Fred J. Maroon
(*Right*) © Jack Novak, Photri
62: © William Kulik, Photri
63: © John Aikins, Uniphoto
64: (*Top*) National Museum of American History
(*Bottom*) The White House

World Book Encyclopedia, Inc. offers a wide range of educational and reference materials, including a video—"How to Study." This 45-minute VHS tape combines the appeal of television with an easy-to-use formula for developing successful study habits. For more information on World Book's "How to Study" video, as well as our wide selection of educational and reference books, please write:

World Book Encyclopedia, Inc.
P.O. Box 3405, Chicago, Illinois 60654-9980.